CHINESE MOTIFS
IN CONTEMPORARY DESIGN

CHINESE MOTIFS IN CONTEMPORARY DESIGN

EDITED & PUBLISHED BY SendPoints Publishing Co., Ltd.

PUBLISHER: Lin Gengli

PUBLISHING DIRECTOR: Lin Shijian

CHIEF EDITOR: Lin Shijian

LEAD EDITOR: Lin Qiumei

EXECUTIVE EDITOR: Qiaomei Xian Claire Wei

ART DIRECTOR: Lin Shijian

EXECUTIVE ART EDITOR: Ho Waikin

PROOFREADING: Sundae Li

REGISTERED ADDRESS: Room 15A Block 9 Tsui Chuk Garden, Wong Tai Sin, Kowloon, Hong Kong

TEL: +852-35832323 / **FAX:** +852-35832448

OFFICE ADDRESS: 7F, 9th Anning Street, Jinshazhou, Baiyun District, Guangzhou, China

TEL: +86-20-89095121 / **FAX:** +86-20-89095206

BEIJING OFFICE: Room 107, Floor 1, Xiyingfang Alley, Ande Road, Dongcheng District, Beijing, China

TEL: +86-10-84139071 / **FAX:** +86-10-84139071

SHANGHAI OFFICE: Room 307, Building 1, Hong Qiang Creative Zhabei District, Shanghai, China

TEL: +86-21-63523469 / **FAX:** +86-21-63523469

SALES MANAGER: Sissi

TEL: +86-20-81007895

EMAIL: overseas01@sendpoints.cn

WEBSITE: www.sendpoints.cn / www.spbooks.cn

ISBN 978-988-77573-4-4

Printed and bound in China

Second printing

AMAZING 1983ASIA
EXHIBITION
視覺設計展
臺灣國立高雄應用科技大學藝文中心
2016.12.29-2017.2.10
亚
洲

奇幻
亚洲
AMAZING 1983ASIA
EXHIBITION
視覺設計展

EXHIBITION
視覺設計展
奇幻
亚洲
AMAZING 1983ASIA
EXHIBITION
視覺設計展
2016.12.29-2017.2.10

奇幻
亚洲
AMAZING 1983ASIA
EXHIBITION
視覺設計展

EXHIBITION
視覺設計展
奇幻
亚洲
AMAZING 1983ASIA
EXHIBITION
視覺設計展
臺灣國立高雄應用科技大學藝文中心
2016.12.29-2017.2.10

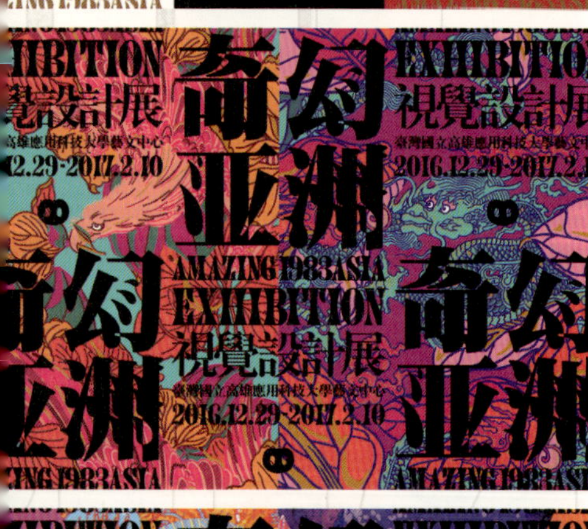
奇幻
亚洲
AMAZING 1983ASIA
EXHIBITION
視覺設計展
2016.12.29-2017.2.10

奇幻
亚洲
AMAZING 1983ASIA
EXHIBITION
視覺設計展
臺灣國立高雄應用科技大學藝文中心
2016.12.29-2017.2.10

奇幻
亚洲
AMAZING 1983ASIA
EXHIBITION

奇幻
亚洲

YAO & SU SU

1983 ASIA

1983ASIA was co-founded by Su Su (Tianjin, China) and YAO (Malaysia) in Shenzhen, China in 2012. They are members of International Association of Designers (IAD). Being among the top-100 Chinese designers in the world, they are also active participators in international cultural and design exchanges.

Their works have been elected to "The Tokyo Type Directors Club" (TDC) and have joint exhibitions in Moscow, Berlin, St Petersburg, Tokyo and Taiwan. In 2016, their branding projects for "HAAIC" and "Yuk Choy High School" won the Steel Award in A'Design Award and Competition (Italy international design award). Their works have been featured in many influential publications such as *Creative Talk in Asia, Asia-Pacific Design, 25 Creative Studios From Across Asia Pacific, Gallery, BranD*, etc.

The mystery and beauty of Oriental Motifs

Different cultural ethnic groups live in their own comfort zones with specific climate, ecology, language, belief, humanity and life. As time and space change, the zones got pulled closer to each other, and people are losing the sense of isolation. We accept each other's existence actively or passively, learning to communicate with each other, and struggling to blend in each other's cultural systems.

We are living in the story named "the Orientals".

The blending of different cultures does not bring about complete convergence. Deep down in the souls of the Orientals, there has always been an urge to rise and shine run out of the "dream".

We never forget the familiar fairy tales that we have enjoyed since our childhood and the bright patterns on the package of joss sticks and candles for ancestor worship. The images of Dragon and Phoenix Bringing Prosperity, Qilin Bringing the Talented Son, the Eight Immortals Crossing the Sea, etc. are all part of the Oriental culture imprinted our minds. The philosophy behind the stories such as the Orient, the Great bird and the Snake, and the War between Fire and Water somehow coincide with the modern scientific concept of circulation. The "dragon and phoenix" pattern has similar elements with the pattern involving the story of the Great bird and the Snake, yet they present greatly different images. Can we perceive the prevalent "auspicious symbols" as people's wish for harmony and unity? Is the "dragon and phoenix" pattern a hope for prosperity, given its historical background and cultural connotations? In familiar Chinese idioms such as "Five Ridges and Six Beasts" and "Beast in Human Attire", can we see the origins

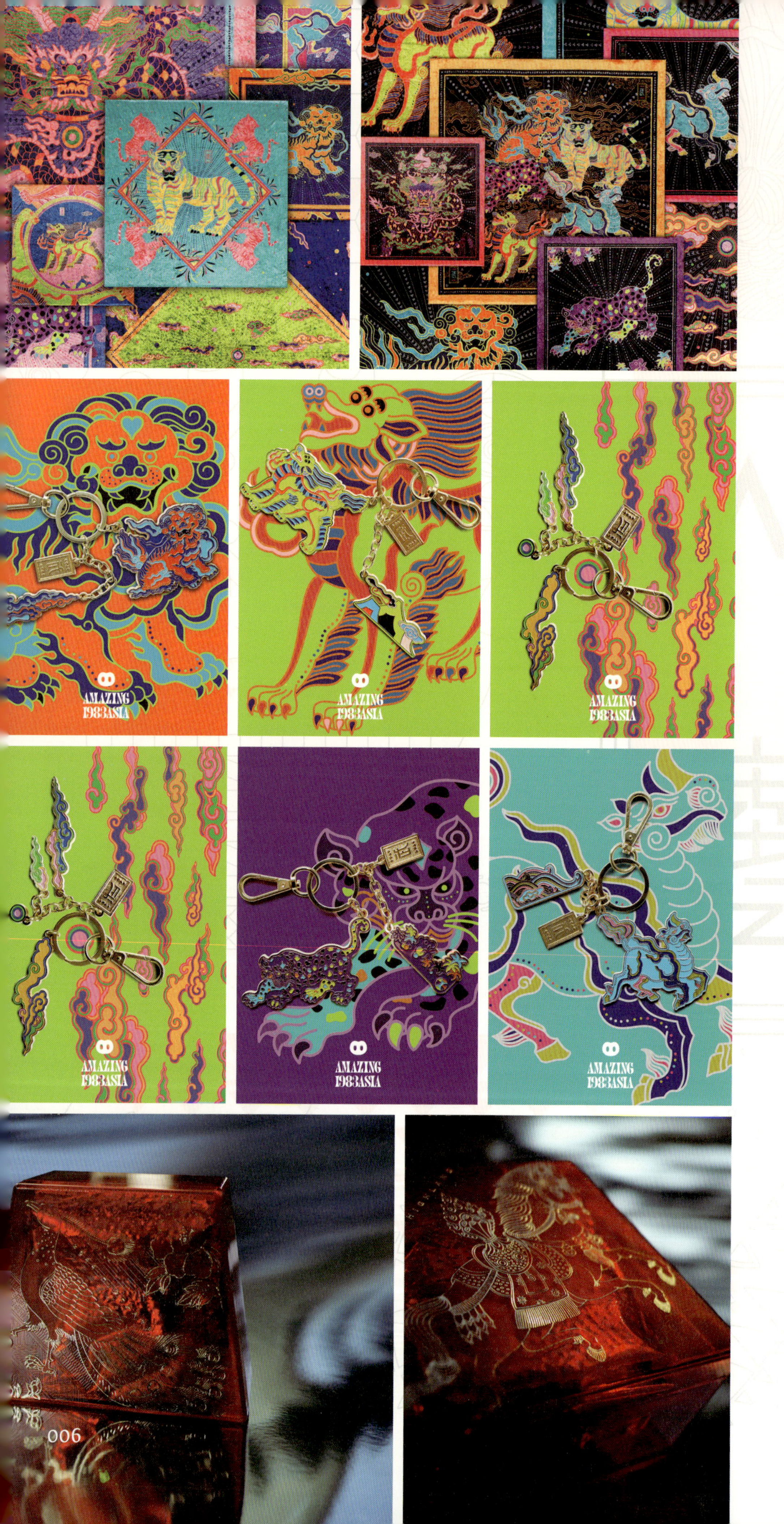
AMAZING
1983ASIA
AMAZING
1983ASIA
AMAZING
1983ASIA
AMAZING
1983ASIA
AMAZING
1983ASIA
AMAZING
1983ASIA

of them as the mythical creatures with different features from a variety of animals? How many totems worshipped by the Orientals?

Every living thing has a soul. In the ancient times, human learned to get along with nature at the dark of the night. India's life tree is believed to have given birth to all animals including human beings. The minority Miao Chinese once believed the Mother Butterfly bred the ancestors of all mankind and taught them to love and care for other living things. From legends told by the bonfire to the mesmerizing fairy tales written by Pu Songling, we discovered a world that transcends time and space. With the reach of technology, we are losing the sense of awe for nation in our heart.

With our curiosity and thirst for knowledge, we are taking in all the information and messages in our own Oriental culture while constantly searching for new domains.

"Tracing the origins" does not mean "advocating restoration" or building "an isolated zone". It confirms the equal identity we have achieved in our communication.

Regardless our different cultural backgrounds, we are equal. The cultural genes in our blood is the source of our wisdom and artistic charm. In the face of our cultural genes, perhaps science is only but one way of understanding the universe.

There are hidden stories in the words of the Orientals and culture in their life.

We encourage designers to observe the Oriental culture with a humble heart, and explore the possibilities of sharing it with the world through "design". What really matters is not how you present it but whether you manage to convey the true Oriental culture we are proud of.

Sometimes we wonder if it would make a difference, if the concept of "design" is originated from the Oriental world.

It is often said that culture, art, commerce and design are inseparable with each other, and there is no clear boundary in between. What makes a design outstanding is the heart and effort one puts in it. The design that is nurtured by culture and I believe it is a noble cause to pursue design works that are nurtured by the great Oriental culture to inspire sincerity at heart and passion in life.

CONTENTS

THE FACIAL MAKE-UP IN CHINESE OPERA

The facial make-up in Chinese opera, or Lian Pu, is known as an icon of traditional Chinese. It refers to the facial designs for Jing and Chou roles. Different types of facial make-ups represent different identities, status, personality and appearance of the characters. As an impressionistic and exaggerated art, the types of facial make-up in Chinese opera is featured by painting brows, eyelids and jowls in various patterns such as bat, swallow wings and butterfly wings. The art of facial make-up is now used in buildings, product packaging, porcelain and costume design.

Eyebrows

His eyes were like that of a phoenix's and his majestic eyebrows resembled silkworms.

Color

Red indicates devotion, courage, bravery, uprightness and loyalty. Guan Yu was famed for his loyalty to his Emperor, Liu Bei.

Beard

A long beard gives the old warrior a solemn and dignified appearance.

关　羽 Guan Yu

Guan Yu, courtesy name Yunchang, was a general serving under the warlord Liu Bei in the late Eastern Han dynasty. Ranked first among the five Tiger Generals, he was respected as the epitome of loyalty and righteousness. He is depicted as a tall, red-skinned man dressed in a green robe, alluding to his legendary portrayal.

Types of facial make-up

(Red) Full Face—The whole face (except for the eyebrows, nose and mouth) painted in the same color is called a full face. Since the color red is used, Guan Yu's facial make-up is called (Red) Full Face.

Forehead

The bar-shaped brows and smiling eyes resemble a butterfly.

Color

Black symbolizes roughness and fierceness. The black face indicates an impartial and selfless personality.

Beard

The exaggerated beard suggests his bold and uninhibited character.

Center of the Forehead

There is a narrow strip from the top of the forehead to the tip of the nose. The strip intersects with the line of the eye sockets to form a cross.

Facial Features

The seemingly smily face with an angry look depict the true disposition of Zhang Fei. His round eyes, and well-formed forehead present him as a loyal and formidable warrior.

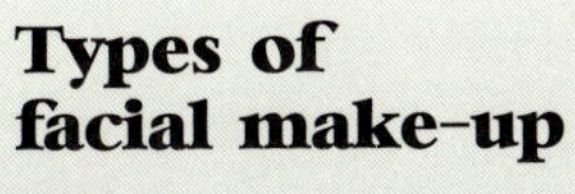

Types of facial make-up

The Cross Face (black cross butterfly face)—a type of facial make-up evolved from the Three-Tile Face. The principal color symbolizing the nature of the character is a narrow strip from the top of the forehead to the tip of the nose. This strip intersects the line of the eye sockets to form a cross, hence the name.

张 飞 Zhang Fei

Zhang Fei was a general served under the warlord Liu Bei in the late Eastern Han dynasty and early Three Kingdoms period. His bravery and might was praised as second only to Guan Yu, He was also described as a cruel and merciless figure to his adversary. *Romance of the Three Kingdoms* depicts him in a positive tone but his short temper and alcohol abuse caused his downfall.

Eyebrows

The shape of the eyebrow resembles that of a moth. The white eyebrows and the deep red color beneath the eyebrows create a strong contrast.

Nose

Red straight nose.

Color

Red indicates devotion, courage, bravery, uprightness and loyalty, often used to depict old generals with high prestige.

Beard

The white beard is a sign of old age.

*The red face and white beard of Huang Gai suggest that he is a faithful old general.

黄　盖 Huang Gai

Huang Gai was a general under the warlord Sun Quan in the late Eastern Han dynasty. He previously served under Sun Quan's predecessors. At the Battle of Chi Bi, together with Zhou Yu, he helped deliver the "Last Resort" plan. After being "attacked" by Zhou Yu, Huang Gai surrendered to Cao Cao, where he then set fire to the Wei fleet, leading to a great victory for Wu.

Types of facial make-up

Six-Tenth Face—a type of facial make-up developed from the Full Face. The principal color occupies about six tenths of the face. The rest of the forehead is taken up by the enlarged white eyebrows, which occupy about four tenths of the face.

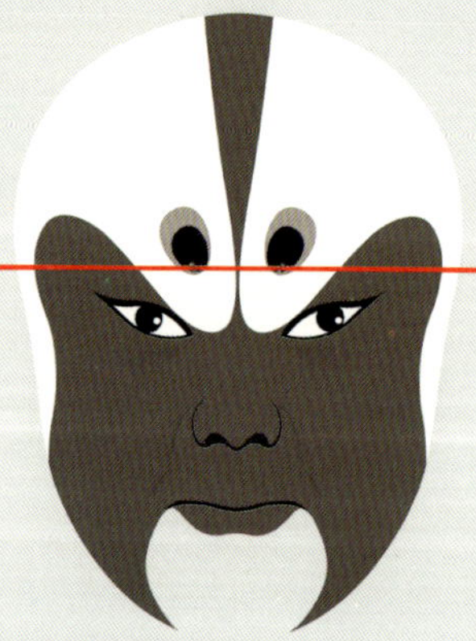

Color

Blue, similar to green facial make-up is often used for characters described as fierce, courageous and resolute.

Forehead

The oval mirror and cloud pattern represents Lei Zhenzi's celestial image.

Eyes

Pointed eyes with the eye corners extended upward presents the fierce look of the character.

Mouth

A pointed mouth (the mouth of the thunder god).

Types of facial make-up

Flower Three-Tile Face—a type of facial make-up in Peking Opera evolved from the Three-Tile Face. It has intricate, variegated designs around the eyes, brows and nose, indicating a multiple personality.

雷震子 Lei Zhenzi

Lei Zhenzi is a character featured in the famed classic Chinese novel *Fengshen Yanyi*. He is a celestial being created by a certain great thunderstorm who then became an adopted son of King Wen of the Zhou dynasty. In the novel, he is depicted as a man with a blue face, red hair, bright eyes and irregular teeth. With a golden rod as his weapon, he served with distinction in the war of King Wu's conquest over Yin.

后 羿
Hou Yi

Hou Yi is a mythological Chinese archer. He is portrayed as a god of archery. The facial make-up of Houyi adopts a Three-Tile Pattern. The red color suggests a loyal and integrity character, and the nine yellow circles on the facial make-up represent the nine suns that he shot down.

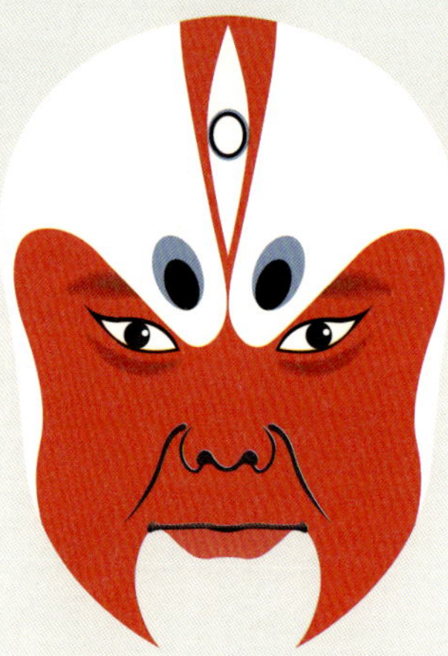

闻 仲
Wen Zhong

Wen Zhong is a character in the classic Chinese novel *Fengshen Yanyi*. He is a high-ranking official under King Da Yi in the story. The facial make-up adopts a red Six-Division Pattern. There is a third eye atop his forehead that sees through any level of disillusion and falsehood. The main color of the facial make-up is red and white, representing a loyalty and integrity character.

陈 奇
Chen Qi

Chen Qi is a character in the classic Chinese novel *Fengshen Yanyi*. He is believed to be able to breath out yellow clouds to kill the enemy. The facial make-up features red as the main color. It adopts a red Three-Tile Pattern, representing a loyal and integrity character.

郑 伦
Zheng Lun

Zheng Lun is a character featured in the famed Chinese novel *Fengshen Yanyi*, he is one of the deity of "Generals Heng and Ha" (哼哈二将). He could shoot two jets of white color gas from his nostrils to suck in one's soul. The facial make-up features green as the main color, reflecting his bravery and irascibility.

崇侯虎

Chong Houhu

Chong Houhu is a character featured in the Chinese novel *Fengshen Yanyi*. He is one of the four Grand Dukes in the Shang Dynasty. The main color of his facial make-up is water-white, suggesting his cunning and a suspicious nature.

崇黑虎

Chong Heihu

Chong Heihu is a character featured in the famed classic Chinese novel *Fengshen Yanyi*. He is the younger brother of Chong Houhu. The facial make-up uses black as the base color, indicating the character's integrity and uprightness.

土行孙

Tu Xingsun

Tu Xingsun is a character featured in the famed classic Chinese novel *Fengshen Yanyi*. He is a dwarf general with special abilities in the opera "Three Mountain Pass". The yellow Three-Tile Pattern suggests a brave and fierce character.

程咬金

Cheng Yaojin

Cheng Yaojin is a character in the Chinese classics *Romance of Sui and Tang Dynasties*. There is a popular Chinese saying called "Cheng Yaojin shows up suddenly in the way". It describes a situation where someone shows up unexpectedly and disrupts a plan. The color of his facial make-up is green, representing bravery and irascibility.

牛 邈
Niu Miao

姚 刚
Yao Gang

苏 献
Su Xian

马 武
Ma Wu

庞 统
Pang Tong

周 仓
Zhou Cang

魏 延
Wei Yan

孟 达
Meng Da

严 颜
Yan Yan

姜 尚
Jiang Shang

钟离春
Zhong Lichun

里 克
Li Ke

毛 贲
Mao Bi

魏 绛
Wei Jiang

颖考叔
Ying Kaoshu

先 篾
Xian Miao

屠岸贾
Tu Angu

须 贾
Hui Gu

专 诸
Zhuan Zhu

姬 僚
Ji Liao

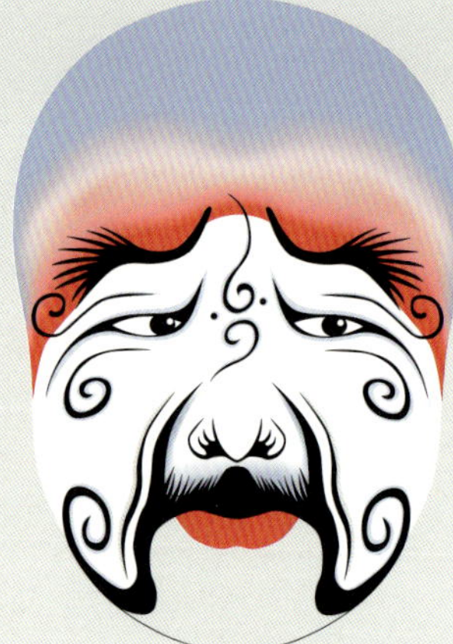

米南洼
Mi Nanwa

李 刚
Li Gang

廉 颇
Lian Po

伊 利
Yi Li

胡 伤
Hu Shang

荆 轲
Jing Ke

赵 高
Zhao Gao

王 陵
Wang Ling

英 布
Ying Bu

项 羽
Xiang Yu

彭 越
Peng Yue

马 通
Ma Tong

铫 期
Yao Qi

吴 汉
Wu Han

郭 荣
Guo Rong

王 元
Wang Yuan

姜 维
Jiang Wei

曹 操
Cao Cao

张 苞
Zhang Bao

邓 艾
Deng Ai

沙摩柯
Sha Moke

典 韦
Dian Wei

夏侯淳
Xiahou Chun

夏侯渊
Xiahou Yuan

夏侯德
Xiahou De

许 诸
Xu Zhu

曹 洪
Cao Hong

张 颌
Zhang He

徐 晃
Xu Huang

孟 潭
Meng Tan

蔡 阳
Cai Yang

孔 秀
Kong Xiu

秦 琪
Qin Qi

司马懿
Sima Yi

司马师
Sima Shi

郭 淮
Guo Huai

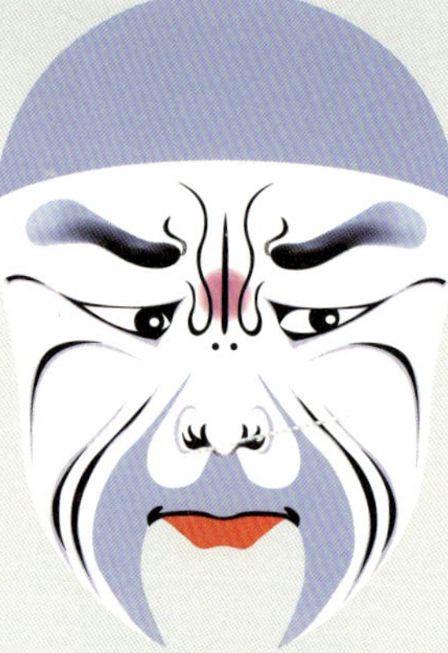

董 卓
Dong Zhuo

马 谡
Ma Su

程 普
Cheng Pu

孙 权
Sun Quan

吕 蒙
Lv Meng

太史慈
Taishi Ci

蒋 钦
Jiang Qin

凌　统
Ling Tong

周　泰
Zhou Qin

周　处
Zhou Chu

尉迟宝林
Yuchi Baolin

单雄信
Shan Xiongxin

尉迟恭
Yuchi Gong

金　甲
Jin Jia

童　环
Tong Huan

李元霸
Li Yuanba

李 密
Li Mi

杨 林
Yang Lin

新文礼
Xin Wenli

秦 英
Qin Ying

窦一虎
Dou Yihu

薛 刚
Xue Gang

苏宝同
Su Baotong

薛 葵
Xue Kui

安殿宝
An Dianbao

巴　兰
Ba Lan

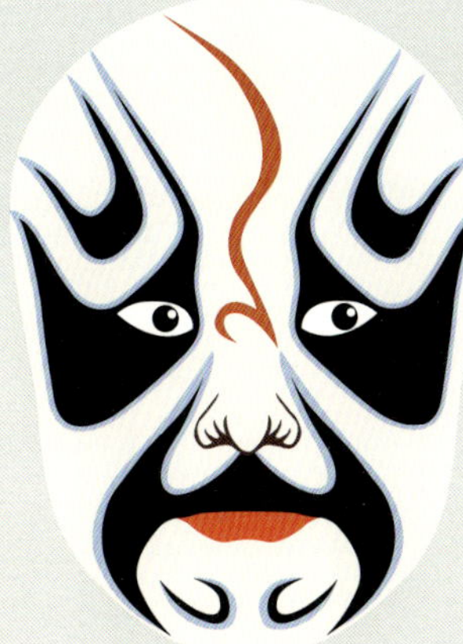
贺天龙
He Tianlong

宇文成都
Yuwen Chengdu

鲍子安
Bao Zian

黄　胖
Huang Pang

猩猩胆
XIng Xing Dan

盖苏文
Gai Suwen

巴　杰
Ba Jie

朱　温
Zhu Wen

孟觉海
Meng Juehai

李克用
Li Keyong

胡 理
Hu Li

王彦章
Wang Yanzhang

周德威
Zhou Dewei

余 洪
Yu Hong

郑子明
Zheng Ziming

呼延赞
Hu Yanzan

崔子健
Cui Zijian

高　旺
Gao Wang

文庆王
Wen Qingwang

韩　昌
Han Chang

白天佐
Bai Tianzuo

孟　良
Meng Liang

焦　赞
Jiao Zan

杨延赞
Yang Yanzan

杨延嗣
Yang Yansi

巴若里
Ba Ruo Li

Peking Opera: The Avengers

The illustration was based on western superhero movies. The designer used the elements in Peking Opera to illustrate the superhero images.

出品：奇妙文化
監製：花望記
領銜主演：
斯蒂夫・羅傑斯
托尼・斯塔克
托爾
布魯斯・班納
娜塔莎・羅曼諾夫
克林特・巴頓
洛基

Daybreak
Illustrator
Fantastic Cultural

We can often find traditional Chinese elements in your works. Why do you often use them in your creation?

••• Someone I respect once told me that "as Chinese designers or illustrators, we have an obligation to promote traditional Chinese culture". His words influenced me a lot.

There are various kinds of traditional Chinese motifs reflecting rich culture connotations. What aspects attract your attention most?

••• I am particularly attracted by Chinese culture of Tang and Song dynasties, especially the Buddhist culture of Tang dynasty.

The illustrations "Peking Opera: The Avengers" feature the elements of Peking Opera facial make-ups. Where did you find the inspiration and how did you put it into practice?

••• After I saw the movie *The Avengers*, I wanted to illustrate the characters in the movie. It seems that many people have the same idea, and I wanted to draw something different. One day when I passed by a Cantonese Opera theatre, it occurred to me that I cloud use the elements of Pecking Opera to draw the characters in Western movies. Then I started the process of this project. And the result turned out to be amazing.

When combining traditional elements into modern design, have you met any difficulties and how did you solve them?

••• I think traditional works emphasizing "artistic conception", while modern designs are more focused on "concrete model". You know it is difficult to visualize the "conception", the only way is to use a three-dimensional way to understand the design elements.

Please share an interesting discovery in your creating process?

••• The most important thing I found in creation is to turn off your WIFI and put your phone away, otherwise you will never get started.

Year of the Monkey "BING SHEN"

This work is both a combination of traditional and modern styles and an integration of Eastern and the Western elements. Camouflage pants and sneakers are examples of modern elements.

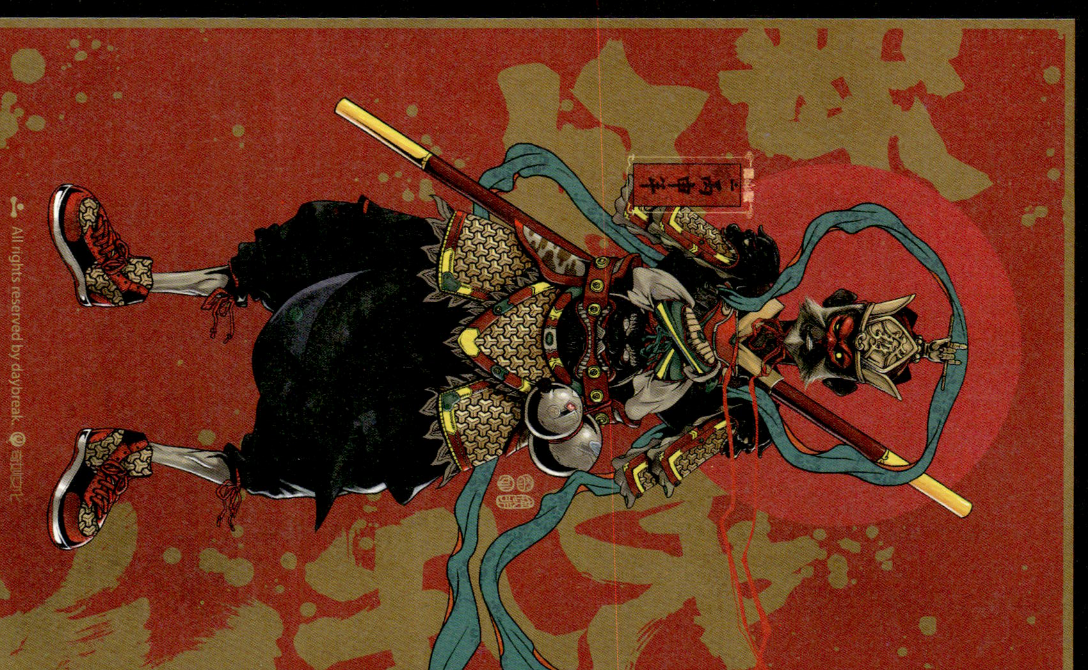

Year of the Fire Rooster "DING YOU"

The expression of "Eyes half shut" indicates our life is like the vicar's egg.

The Poster Exhibiton of Xiazhi Music Festival

The exhibition was held in Shanghai, the designer used Chinese elements to depict a king playing the Chinese lute.

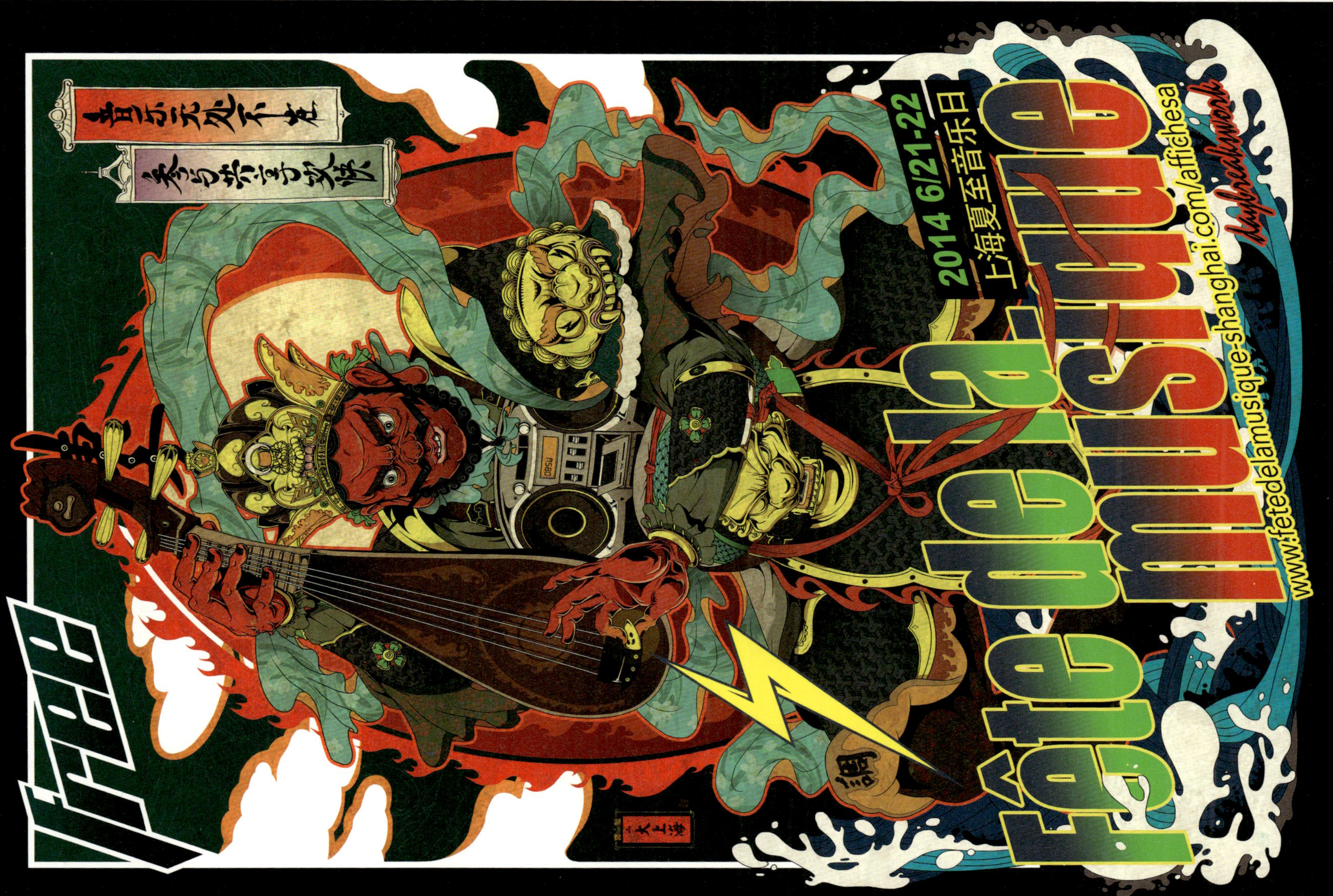

The Three Kingdoms•Romance of Sui and Tang Dynasties

S:
VIM Graphics Design

D:
He Yong
Zhang Hui
Hailong Miao
Ruiji Chu

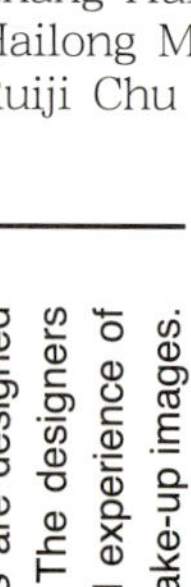

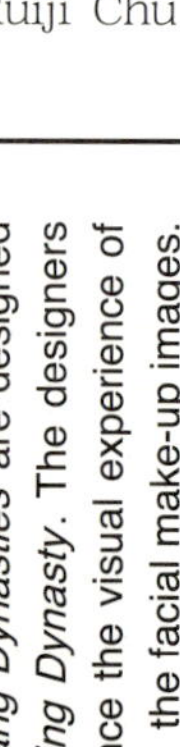

The character prototypes from the books *The Three Kingdoms* and *Romance of Sui and Tang Dynasties* are designed based on ancient Chinese books *One Hundred Portraits of Peking Opera Characters—Qing Dynasty*. The designers visualized and flattened the traditional facial make-ups, and applied vibrant colors to enhance the visual experience of the facial make-up images.

PEKING OPERA
PEKING OPERA
PEKING OPERA
PEKING OPERA

PEKING OPERA

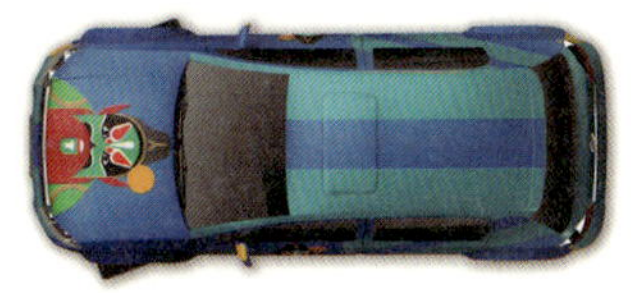

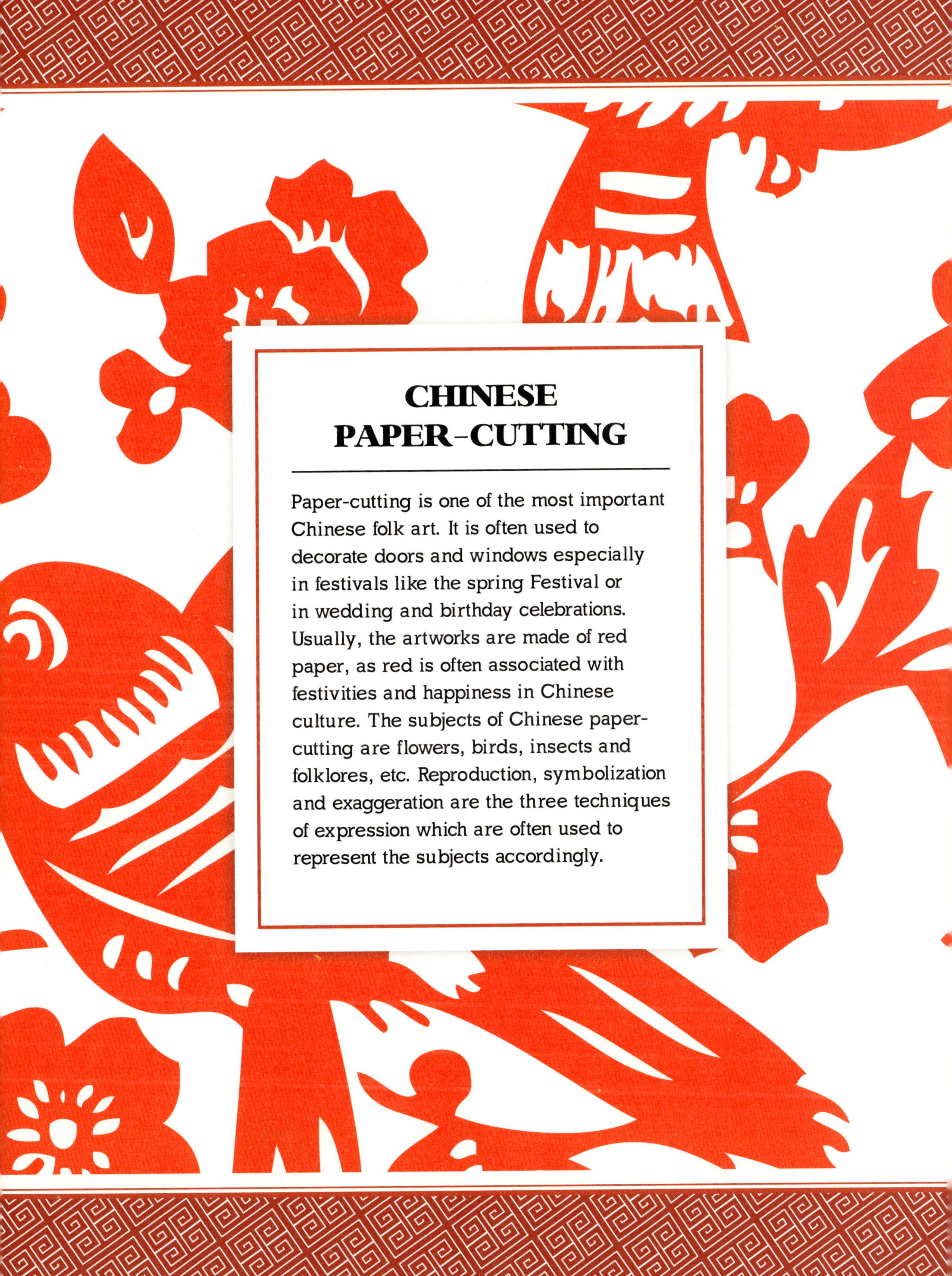

CHINESE PAPER-CUTTING

Paper-cutting is one of the most important Chinese folk art. It is often used to decorate doors and windows especially in festivals like the spring Festival or in wedding and birthday celebrations. Usually, the artworks are made of red paper, as red is often associated with festivities and happiness in Chinese culture. The subjects of Chinese paper-cutting are flowers, birds, insects and folklores, etc. Reproduction, symbolization and exaggeration are the three techniques of expression which are often used to represent the subjects accordingly.

The themes of paper-cutting

The themes of paper-cutting are often based on social customs. During the Chinese New Year, people often put up a poster with the fu character (福 'happiness') to express their wish for a happy life and a good future. The fu poster is often placed upside down intentionally to symbolize the arrival of happiness and luck. Given that in the Chinese language, the pronunciation of the character meaning 'placing upside down' is similar to that of the character for 'arrival'.

Pattern

The symmetry pattern is commonly seen in the art of paper-cutting, presenting a harmonious and solemn feeling.

Elements

The magpie is celebrated as "a bird of great good fortune, of sturdy spirit and a provider of prosperity and development" in traditional Chinese culture. It is often seen as an omen of good fortune.

喜鹊报福

THE MAGPIE DELIVERING GOOD NEWS

Paper-cutting pattern

The Sawtooth Pattern

Depicts harder or pointed objects such as hills or animal hair.

The Crescent Pattern

Represents softer lines or waves such as willow leaves or water waves.

Round Opening Pattern

Depicts round objects such as the stigma of a flower and other decorative elements.

福
吉
祥

福

福

福

福

福

福
福
福
有
福
福
福

鸳鸯戏水

TWO MANDARIN DUCKS PLAYING IN WATER

Subject

This is a design based on social customs. It is often used in weddings to express the wish for love and happiness to new couples.

Pattern

A combination of symmetrical patterns and asymmetric patterns. The symmetrical pattern is done with scissors. And the asymmetric pattern is tailored by scissors or knives.

Elements

1.Mandarin ducks: representing affectionate couples; 2.Peony: a symbol of wealth and honors; 3.Bat: The Chinese character for bat " 蝠 " that sounds identical to the word for good fortune " 福 " fu; 4.Fish: Fish symbolizes wealth as in Chinese the character for fish " 鱼 " yu, sounds like the character " 余 " which means abundance and affulence.

Paper-cutting pattern

Fishscale pattern

Depicts fish or fishlike objects.

Swirl pattern

Used as a decorative motif to represent fur.

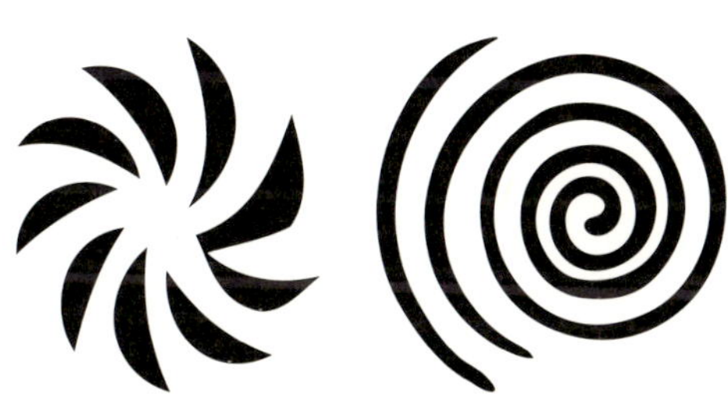

十二生肖

TWELVE CHINESE ZODIAC SIGNS

The Chinese zodiac is a classification scheme that assigns an animal and its reputed attributes to each year in a repeating 12-year cycle. The twelve zodiac signs are: Rat, Ox, Tiger, Rabbit, Dragon, Snake, Horse, Goat, Monkey, Rooster, Dog and Pig. They are closely linked to the Five Chinese Elements: Metal, Wood, Water, Fire and Earth. It is said they are widely associated with a culture of ascribing a person's personality or events in his or her life to the supposed influence of the person's particular relationship to the cycle.

There are three categories of Chinese Zodiac. The first is domesticated animals such as goat, horse, pig, dog and rooster. The second is wild animals such as tiger, snake, monkey and rat. The last one is dragon, a celestial animal which is a symbol of power and good luck. Dragon motif is commonly seen in Chinese paper-cutting art.

Chinese Zodiac symbolism

Rat and Ox
intelligent and diligent

Tiger and Rabbit
brave and prudent

Dragon and Snake
tough and flexible

Horse and Goat
persevering and amiable

Monkey and Chicken
agile and constant

Dog and Pig
loyal and agreeable

舞龙（狮）
DRAGON AND LION DANCE

Dragon and lion dance is a form of traditional dance and performance in Chinese culture. The dance is performed by a team of dancers who mimic a dragon or a lion's movements in a dragon or lion's costume. It is usually performed during the Chinese New Year and other traditional, cultural and religious festivals.

放爆竹
BURNING FIRECRACKERS

It is an important custom to set off firecrackers and fireworks during the Chinese New Year holiday. In traditional Chinese culture, firecrackers were originally used to scare away evil spirits. Now it is a way to create a jubilant atmosphere to the festival that brings great happiness.

抬花轿
LIFTING THE BRIDAL SEDAN CHAIR

Lifting the bridal sedan chair is a traditional Chinese custom in wedding ceremony. Sedan chairs were a popular and main means of transportation in ancient China. Decorated-all-in-red bridal sedan chairs were usually used for weddings to set off the festive and happy atmosphere in a wedding ceremony. Usually, four people or eight people are employed to lift the bridal sedan chair.

Yingfa Wang
Executive Director
Victor Design

Block print and craftsmanship have been applied in the packaging design of Cha Tzu Tang, and this time traditional paper-cutting elements were used, why?

••• Basically, we want to convey a design concept of grace and elegance. Paper-cutting and block print share similar characteristics, while paper-cutting is more exquisite. Besides, we want to promote the traditional art of paper-cutting to enable consumers to feel the effort and love that have been put into the product.

We know that each upgrade of package design aims to better convey the product concept. How do you balance innovation and inheritance in the design?

••• When we are developing a design strategy, we focus not only on visual performance, but also on whether the design effectively conveys the meaning of the brand or product. A good design strategy should be both creative and relevant. Therefore, we should analyze the brand image and master the design style first, and then come up with a proper design strategy.

生
龍
虎
活
茶籽堂
cha tzu tang

壽
比
山
南
茶籽堂
cha tzu tang

生
龍
虎
活
闖過一關又一關，別忘了
犒賞，珍愛自己，再往下個高峰邁進

壽
比
山
南

Cha Tzu Tang Gift Sets

Considering this is a high-end camellia oil brand in Taiwan, the packaging design was based on traditional paper-cutting totems and auspicious words meaning luck and longevity.

What factors do you think should be considered when applying traditional elements in modern design?

••• The redesign of traditional elements is important. In other words, we should not simply copy the traditional elements. In Victor Brand Corporation, we build "a strategy model of triangulation" to help our team think better. We know that every brand is unique, so we focus on the core advantage of each brand and customize a specific cultural symbol for the brand, helping them to establish a unique brand image.

How did you achieve such a perfect combination of modern and traditional element in your design involving Chinese paper-cutting?

••• Well, we think it involves three factors: the communication of design concept, the development of traditional craftsmanship and the planning of design objective. The use of traditional paper-cutting totems as the main visual design elements and the auspicious Chinese characters as an auxiliary pattern emphasize a warm atmosphere. The packaging embodies Chu Tzu Tang's original, ecologically friendly image. This most natural present conveys the true spirit of the product.

Dragon Beard Candy and Beauty's Eyes Cake

Tradition has it that Dragon Beard Candies and Beauty's Eyes Cakes are delicate pastries elaborately made by royal chef in Qing dynasty (1616-1912). Traditional Chinese paper-cutting motif combined textile thread were used in the packaging, adding a tranquil and elegant atmosphere to the design.

There are various kinds of traditional Chinese motifs reflecting rich culture connotations. What aspects attract your attention most?

••• Generally, we divide the types of traditional artworks into three groups, i.e., scenery description, objects description and free sketch painting. The craftsmanship and artistic style applied in the traditional artworks are quite charming. The important thing is to translate those public and resonate oriental cultural symbols into an exclusive and brand specific culture symbol. Above all, the designers should understand the traditional oriental motifs and choose a relevant theme, then use their creativity to perfect the design.

Typographic Design

D:
Alice Zong

The red Chinese paper-cutting is a symbol of joy and happiness. The designer added this element into 26 English letters with delicate Chinese impressionistic style and the main color of Chinese red to present the exquisite side of Chinese culture.

Font
of Chinese Papercut

The Brochure of Chinese Folk Culture Villages & Splendid China

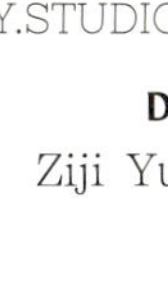

S:
Y.STUDIO

D:
Ziji Yu

The bright colors and distinct graphic design grab immediate attention from the consumers. The use of Chinese paper cutting and window lattice motifs as an auxiliary pattern emphasizes the brand's focus on Chinese Folk Culture Villages & Splendid China.

NEW YEAR PAINTING

New Year paintings is an art form in Traditional Chinese folk culture. The paintings are called "New Year paintings" because they are mostly posted during the New Year holiday for decoration and they are also a symbol of New Year's greetings. When Chinese New Year arrives, every family post new paintings in their homes. These paintings often covers four main themes: the immortals and mascots, the secular life, babies and beauties, stories and myths.

连年有余

LOTUS AND FISHES

The pattern is made up of lotus flower and koi fish. It was used on the decoration of objects in Qing dynasty, meaning "rich and have a surplus" every year.

A baby face with a Buddha body

The combination of "baby face" and "Buddha body" means a family's hope for the Buddha to illuminate.

Koi fish

In traditional Chinese folk culture, people pray for a rich and surplus life. The fish has the same pronunciation of " 余 " and " 裕 " which means abundance and affluence. Therefore, fish is a powerful symbol of strength and perseverance.

Lotus Flower

Lotus has often been used as a symbolic plant in both religious and cultural context. It represents divinity and non-attachment. The lotus flower motif is usually used in apparel and utensil designs.

As a god who brings wealth and affluence, the God of Wealth is worshiped by most Chinese. In the Spring Festival, every family posts a picture of the god for his blessings. The God of Wealth is usually painted in the image of civilian officials.

Color of New Year Paintings

The color of New Year paintings is mainly red to create a happy and festive atmosphere. Yangliuqing in Tianjin, China is the most famous production location for New Year paintings. Most of these paintings feature rich and bright colors with sharp contrasts.

民间文财神

THE GOD OF WEALTH

Elements

Fu Wa

The hope to have many children.

Peony

A symbol of prosperity and glory.

Sika deer

In ancient China, an official's salary are called "俸禄" fenglu. The pronunciation of Chinese character "鹿" lu sounds identical to the word for salary "禄".

Fan Sheng

Originally used as headwear, then it also used in garments, jade jewelry and worship ceremony, etc.

Qi Lin

The qilin or kirin is a mythical hooved chimerical creature known in Chinese and other East Asian culture. It is a good omen thought to occasion prosperity or serenity.

Jue (vessel)

A jue is a shape of Chinese ritual bronze, a tripod vessel or goblet used to serve or warm wine.

八仙慶壽
日
月
福如東海長流水
壽比南山不老松

財神到

中和

壽

福

神英

鎮宅

Fun 羊 (Ram)

S:
SUMP DESIGN

D:
Zihuai Shen

The designers aim to present the more interesting side of traditional Chinese culture. Frequently seen Spring Festival couplets such as Door God, Money God and so on were applied to decorate the animal "Ram". The designers used the simple geometry sculpts to visualize the strokes in Chinese characters.

2015 Chinese New Year
2015 Chinese New Year

2015
Chinese
New
Year

CREATE WISDOM

D:
Peng Chao

The inspiration of this design is derived from traditional Chinese art. The ball placed above the boy's head is deemed as a symbolic version of the universe, and the image of a boy interacting with the universe with both ease and joy indicates the company values for competency and creativity. The main feature of the design is to convey the company's emphasis on the integration of traditional culture with innovation.

CREATE WISDOM
CREATIVE PRODUCT CENTER

MID–AUTUMN FESTIVAL
CREATIVE PRODUCT CENTER

SPRING FESTIVAL
CREATIVE PRODUCT CENTER

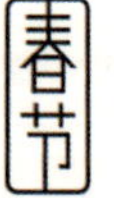

CUSTOMIZATION
CREATIVE PRODUCT CENTER

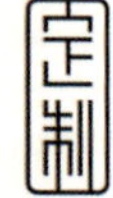

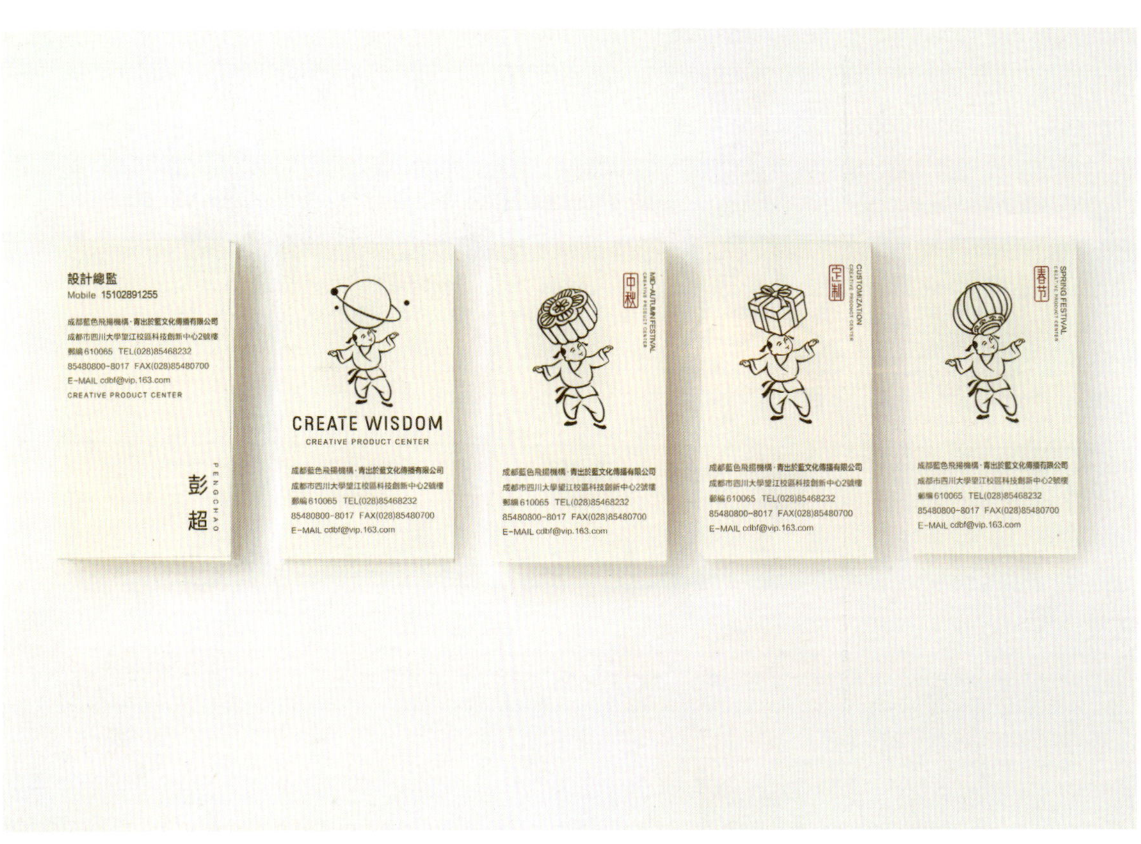
設計總監
Mobile 15102891255
成都藍色飛揚機構·青出於藍文化傳播有限公司
成都市四川大學望江校區科技創新中心2號樓
郵編 610065 TEL(028)85468232
85480800-8017 FAX(028)85480700
E-MAIL cdbf@vip.163.com
CREATIVE PRODUCT CENTER
彭超
PENGCHAO
CREATE WISDOM
CREATIVE PRODUCT CENTER
中秋
MID-AUTUMN FESTIVAL
CREATIVE PRODUCT CENTER
定制
CUSTOMIZATION
CREATIVE PRODUCT CENTER
春节
SPRING FESTIVAL
CREATIVE PRODUCT CENTER

CREATE WISDOM
成都市四川大學望江校區科技創新中心2號樓
郵編 610065 TEL(028)85468232 85480800-8017
FAX(028)85480700 E-MAIL cdbf@vip.163.com
CREATE WISDOM

LIVING WITH GODS

D:
Lee chieh-ting

The designer used the image of gods in Chinese culture to present our own image in modern life. Making these images into familiar symbols in our daily life helps encourage young people to learn about traditional culture.

Cai Shen
the God of money
財 神 ○

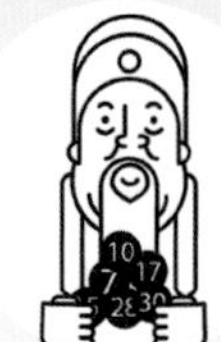

Fu Xing
the God of luck
福 星 ○

Zao Shen
the God of food
灶 神 ◑

Shun Feng Er
the God of sound
順風耳 ○

Lv Dongbin
the God of hair style
呂洞賓 ◑

Yue Lao
the God of love
月 老 ○

Hu Ye
the God of candy
虎 爺 ◑

Wen Chang
the God of exam
文 昌 ●

Yu Lü
the God of door
鬱 壘 ○

Chen Tuan
the God of sleep
陳 摶 ○

Guan Sheng Di Jun
the God of businese
關聖帝君 ●

Shen Shu
the God of door
神 荼 ○

Chuang Mu
the God of sex
床 母 ○

Hua Shen
the God of flower
花 神 ◑

Zhi Nv
the God of weave
織 女 ◑

Lu Ban
the God of tool
魯 班 ●

Cheng Huang Ye
the God of city
城隍爺 ○

Wen Pan Guan
the God of justice
文判官 ○

Wu Pan Guan
the God of punishment
武判官 ○

Wu Dao Zi
the God of painting
吴道子 ●

Guan Yin
the God of message
觀 音 ●

Xuan Tian Shang Di
the God of pork
玄天上帝 ●

Xi Qin Wang Ye
the God of theater
西秦王爺 ◑

Qian Li Yan
the God of sight
千裏眼 ○

Wei Tuo Zun Zhe
the God of speed
韋馱尊者 ●

Tian Du Yuan Shuai
the God of music
天都元帥 ◑

Tai Shang Lao Jun
the God of health food
太上老君 ○

Zhang Shuai
the God of pimple
張 帥 ○

Dian Mu
the God of electricity
電 母 ●

Feng Shen
the God of wind
風 神 ◑

Fa Zhu Zhen Jun
the God of fravel
法主真君 ◑

Hou Ji
the God of crop
後 稷 ○

Bao Sheng Da Di
the God of medical
寶生大帝 ●

Long Wang
the God of water
龍 王 ◑

Yu Bo
the God of rain
雨 伯 ○

He Ye Xian Shi
the God of building
荷葉仙師 ●

Lu Yu
the God of tea
陸 羽 ◑

Ne Zha
the God of car
哪 吒 ●

Nü Wa Niang Niang
the God of repairing
女媧娘娘 ○

Cai Lun
the God of paper
蔡 倫 ●

Du Kang
the God of wine
杜 康 ◑

Jiu Tian Xuan Nü
the God of light
九天玄女 ●

Lei Gong
the God of thunder
雷 公 ○

Sun Bin
the God of shoes
孫 臏 ◑

Zhu Ge Liang
the God of steamed bread
諸葛亮 ○

LIVING WITH GODS

45

SYMBOLS

In chinese religion the gods will bless you if you worship to him. But we dont familiar with gods stories and realize what they are in charge of, for example: which god takes charge of your hair cut ? and which god takes responsibility to your food tasting? let's find out the interesting knowledge of chinese gods!

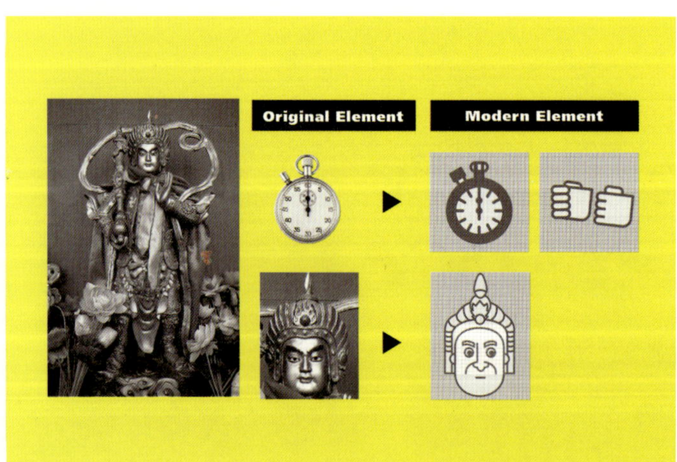

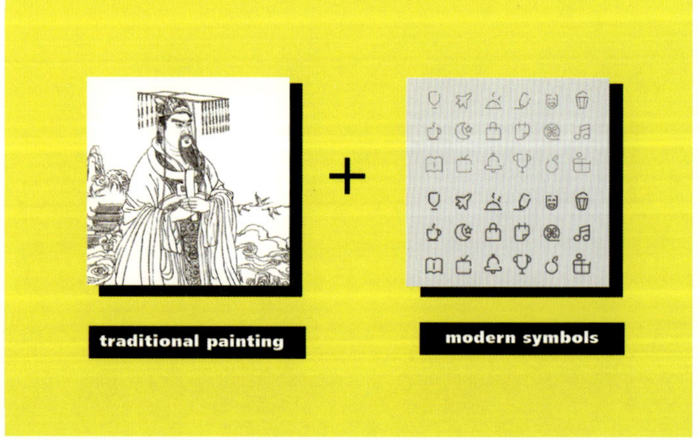

LIVING
WITH

LIVING
WITH
GODS

LIVING
WITH
GODS
Ding mu
the God of electricity

LIVING
WITH
GODS
Shenshu

SYMBOLS

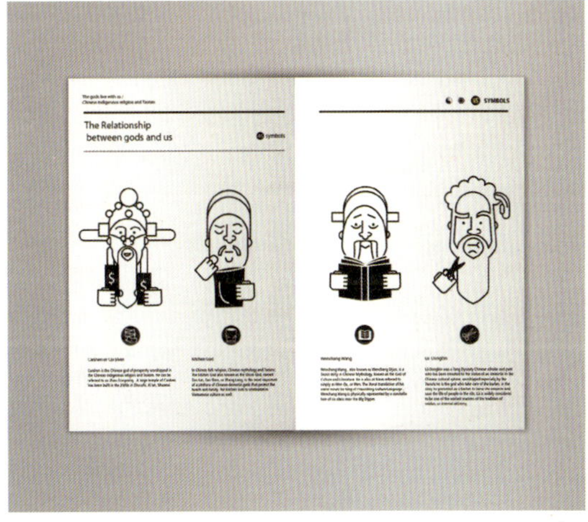
SYMBOLS
The Relationship
between gods and us

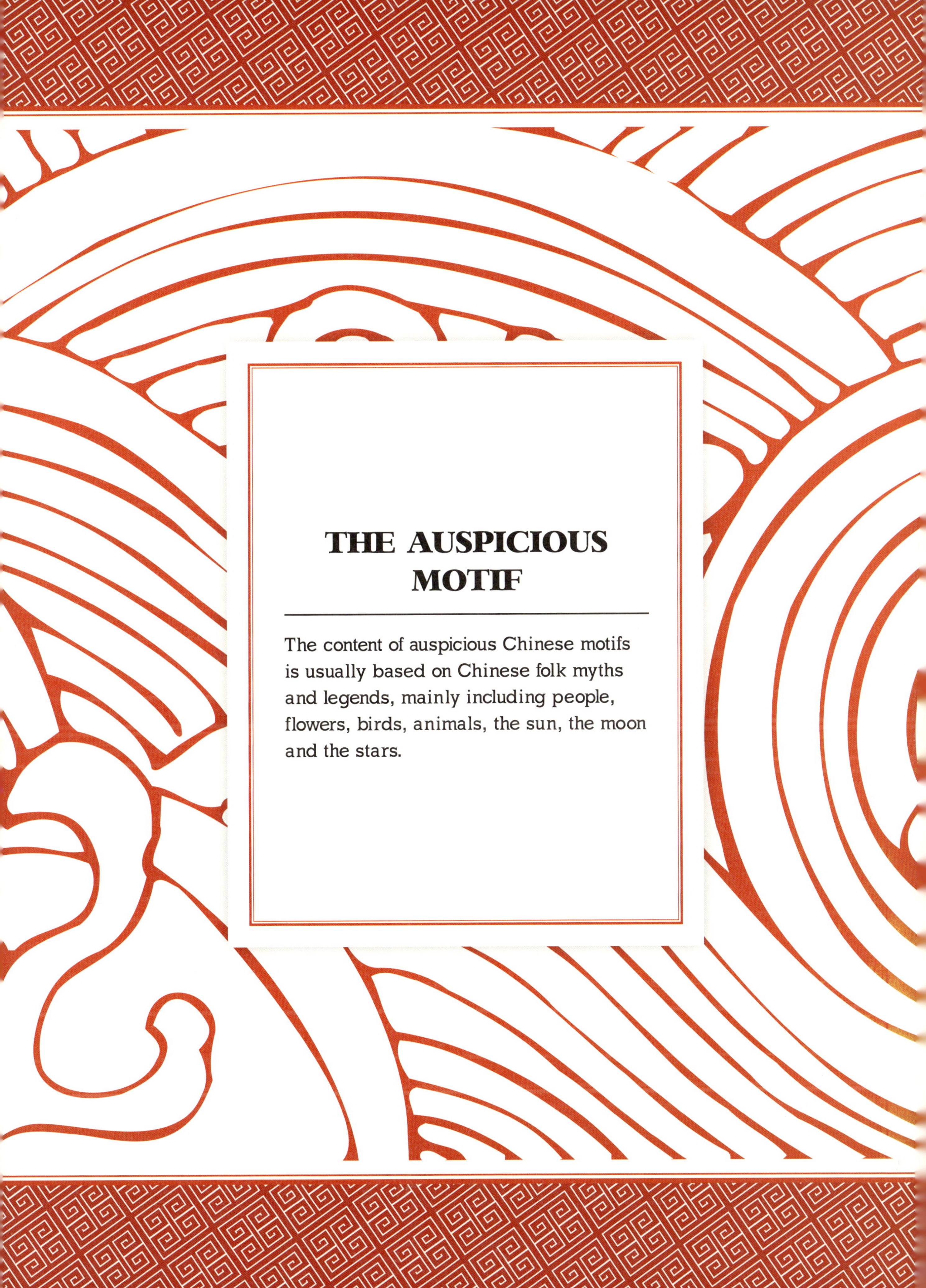

THE AUSPICIOUS MOTIF

The content of auspicious Chinese motifs is usually based on Chinese folk myths and legends, mainly including people, flowers, birds, animals, the sun, the moon and the stars.

The auspicious clouds are described as the clouds that bring luck and peace. It was used as a decoration in ancient building, porcelain and embroidery, etc.

祥 云

AUSPICIOUS CLOUDS

Water has no fixed form. The ripple motif or wave motif features the form of flowing water. It is a traditional motif in porcelain decoration presenting the grandness of ocean water.

水 纹
THE WATER MOTIF

Ripple pattern

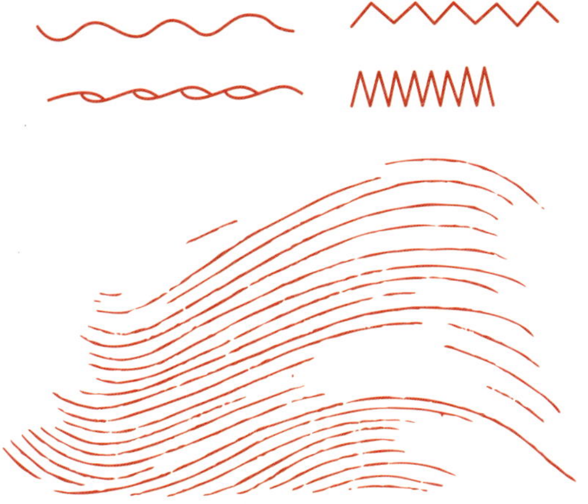

"S"-shaped volute pattern

"C"-shaped volute pattern

Wave pattern

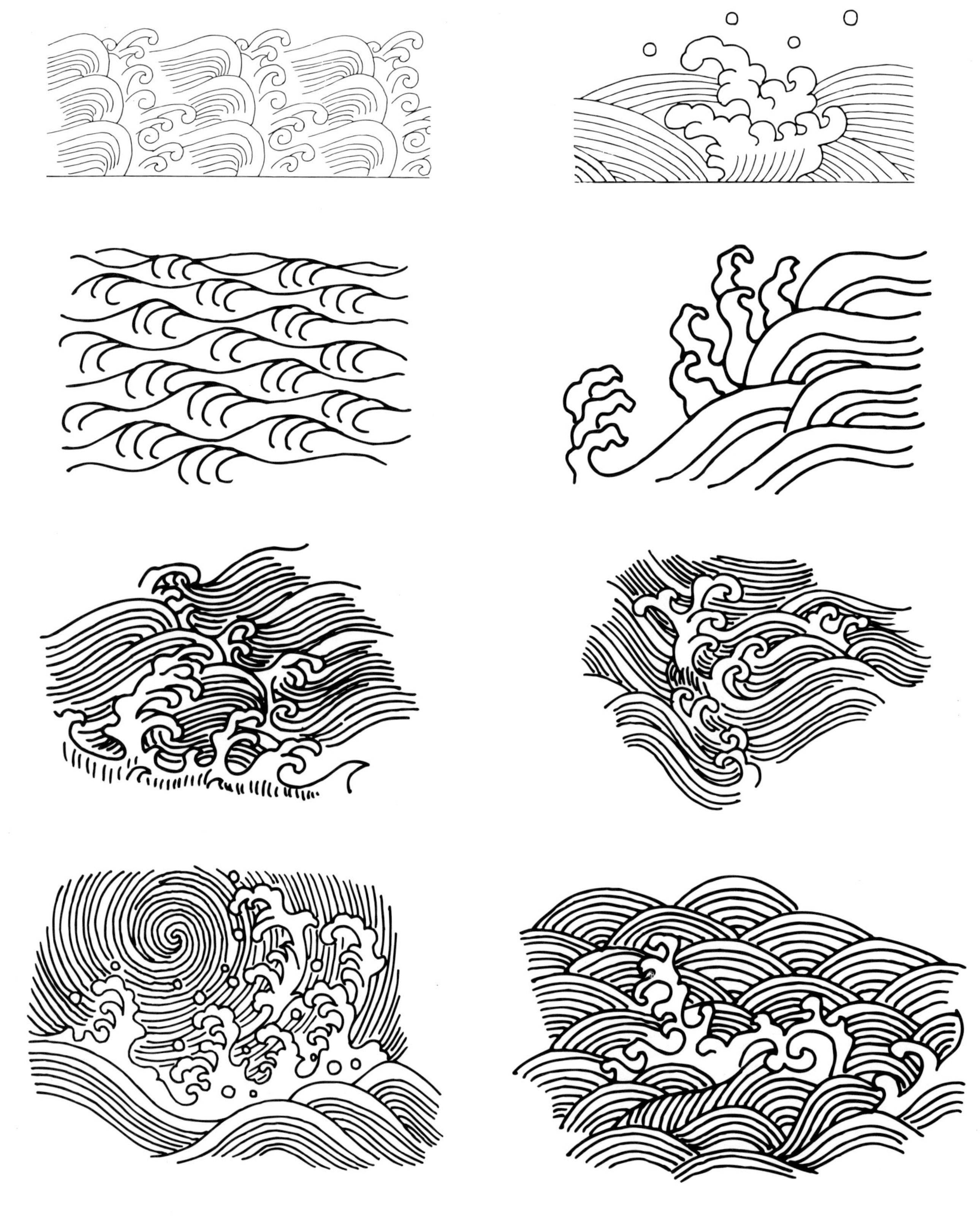

火 纹

THE FIRE MOTIF

The fire motif is regarded as a symbol of the sun. In ancient times, people thought the sun was fire, which encouraged them to worship fire as the great force of the nature. People would often light fire in celebrations and in praying for wealth and happiness. It was most popular in the Chinese Shang and Zhou dynasties. The fire motif now is widely used in architecture and furniture decoration.

Chinese window lattice refers to the decorative pattern inside the window frame, which is a traditional Chinese wooden frame structure. The pattern of Chinese window lattice mainly includes animals and plants, legend figures and geometric patterns, etc. Lines, geometric patterns and various graphs are used in creating the patterns.

窗 棂

CHINESE WINDOW LATTICE

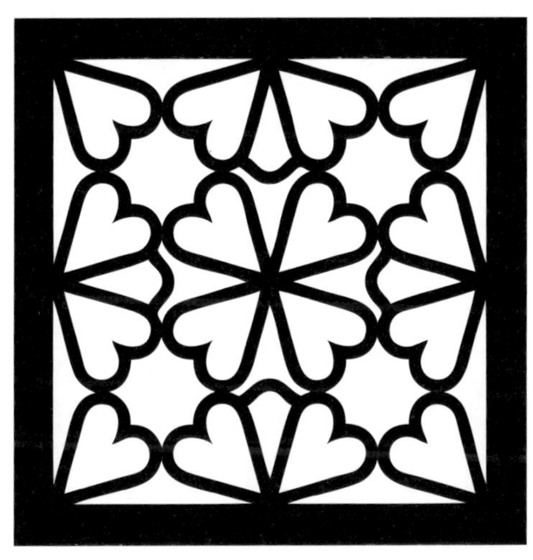

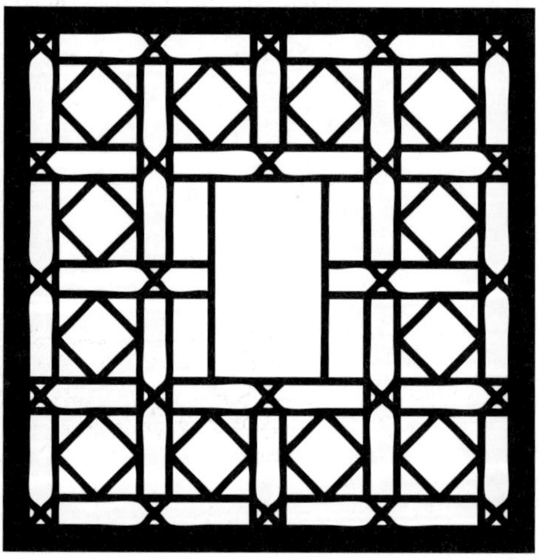

The Chinese character motifs are often used to express people's good wishes. They are usually used on pottery, porcelain, architecture and apparel. Common Chinese character motifs include "卍" (wan), "福" (fu), "寿" (shou), "喜" (xi), etc. "福" fu means happiness and fortune, "寿" shou means longevity and "喜" xi means happiness, etc.

文字纹

THE CHINESE CHARACTER MOTIF

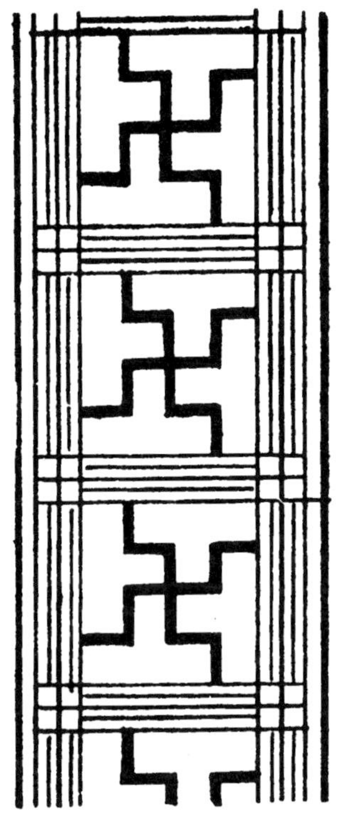

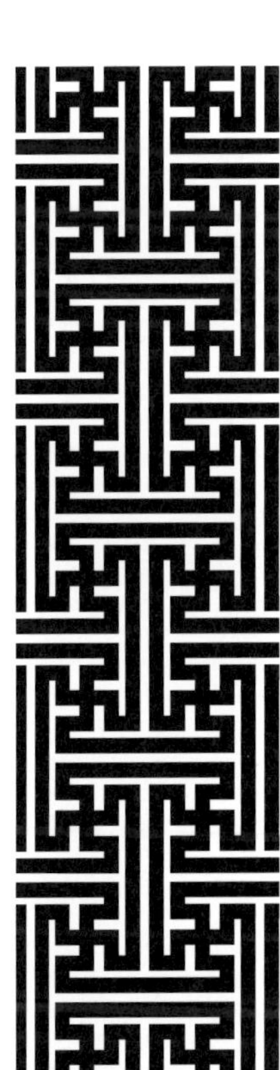

The Fret motif is a popular auxiliary motif used in porcelain decoration. Its Chinese name, hui " 回 " was given because its similar pattern with the Chinese character " 回 " hui. The fret motif is a symbol of endless wealth.

回 纹

THE FRET MOTIF

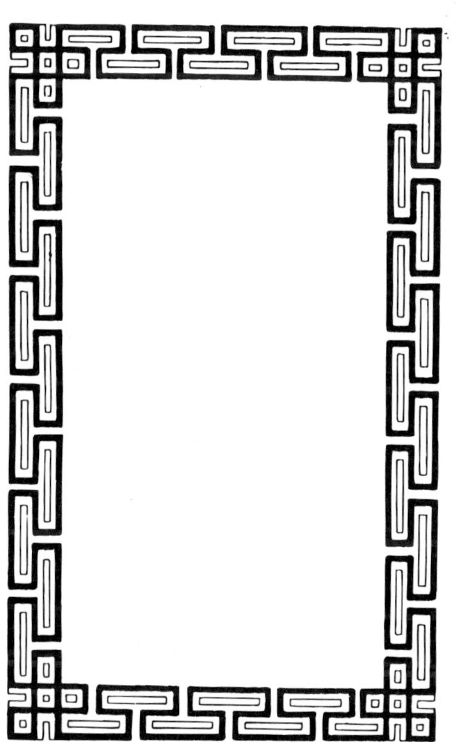

PEKING PIE

PEKING PIE is a souvenir bearing the character of modern Beijing. "Window lattice" elements were used in the packaging design. The designers selected twelve traditional window types to represent twelve landmarks in Beijing.

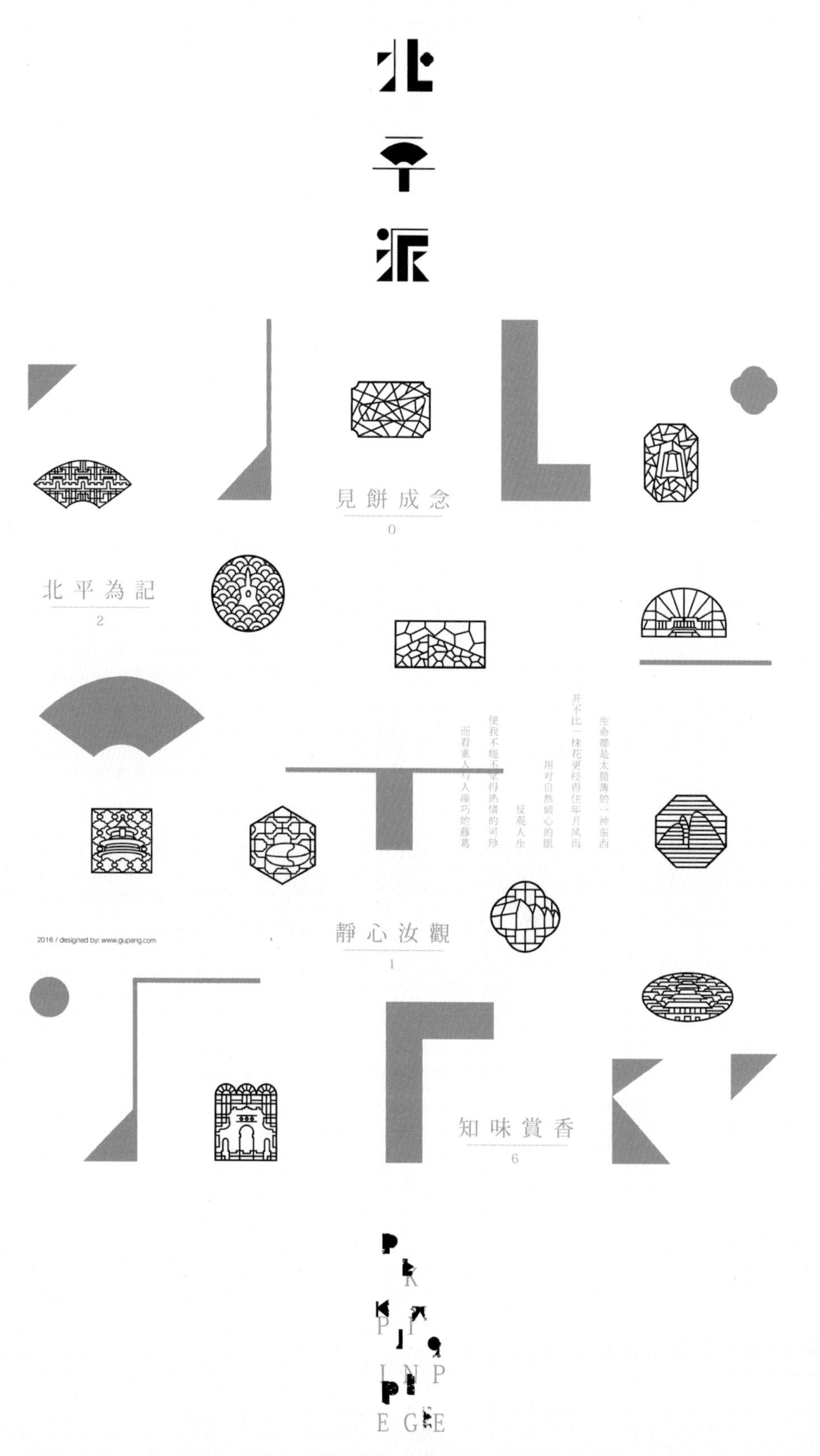

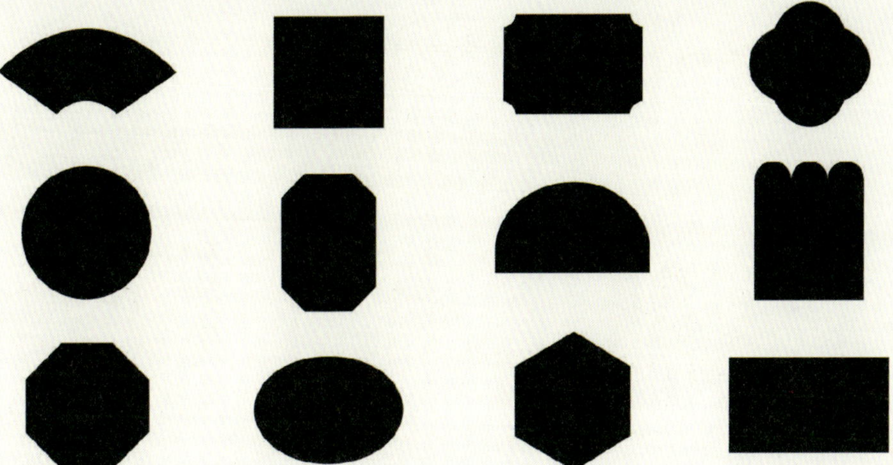

Gu Peng
GUPENG Design

There are various kinds of traditional Chinese motifs reflecting rich culture connotations. What aspects attract your attention most?

••• The personalities and characteristics of oriental people are the aspects that attract me most.

Regarding the packaging of "PEKING PIE", what inspired you to use traditional architecture elements in the design?

••• Beijing is a city where ancient culture and modern civilizations meet. I am impressed by the diversification and inclusiveness of Beijing. Now China is in a transformation era of rebirth. Our economy is developing fast, so is our cultural life. Chinese people are no longer xenophilia as before. Our sense of self-respect is raising, still we are not that confident. China has been deeply influenced by Western culture while reserving a profound culture heritage. We start to get bored of pure vintage style and copinism. We wanted to keep the dignity of oriental culture. There is no doubt that we are the generation who will establish new standards. The designers should shoulder the responsibility of observing the personalities and characteristics of contemporary people.

The window lattice pattern is a combination between traditional window types and modern architectures. How do you balance the two styles?

••• The idea of using window lattice elements came naturally to our minds. We only need to think about the realization method. At first, we used freehand sketching, and then we gave it up because we wanted to express the modernity of Beijing. The final design is a good combination of the city's modern style and rich culture heritage.

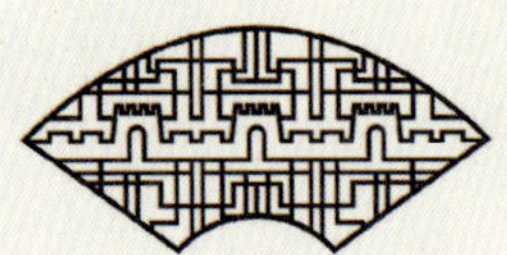

Badaling Great Wall

Temple of Heaven

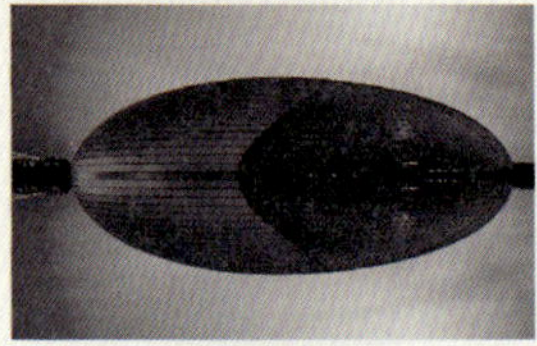

National Centre for the Performing Arts

National Aquatics Center

Beihai Park

CCTV Headquarters

The Great Hall of the People

Tsinghua Campus

Wangjing SOHO

Forbidden City

National Stadium

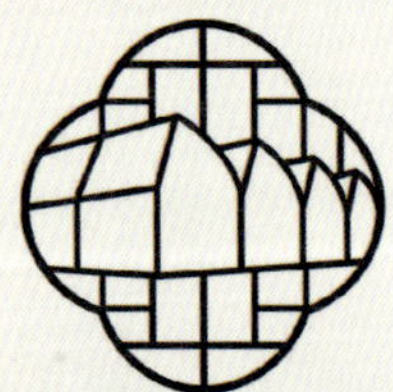

798 Art Zone

The modern architectural shapes integrate into the traditional window forms

The shapes of purposely broken windows, while resembling cookie crumbs, add a sense of warmth and cultural flavor to the design.

What factors do you think should be considered most when applying traditional elements in modern design?

•••Experiencing life itself can help us observe human nature. When using traditional elements in our design, we should consider the context. In the design process of "Peking Pie" packaging, we placed more focus on the visitors travelling to Beijing. It is more important to touch their heart.

In the design process, have you come across any conflicts between different ideas and how do you solve the problem?

•••Actually no, the design process is quite smooth. We three colleagues completed the design together, including selecting architecture pictures, creating the models and using computers to draw the outline. We were all satisfied with the final design.

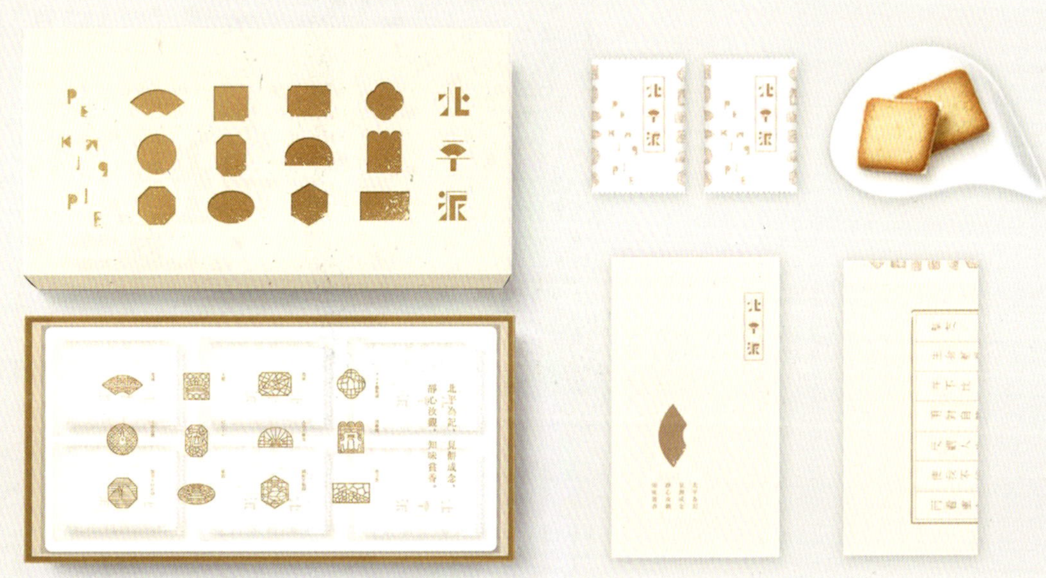

Moon Spring

S:
C&S Brand

Moon spring, which has Zen culture as the background, is committed to a culture temperament as "the quiet mountain pleases the body, the pure water purifies the heart, the spirit satisfies the soul". The 'mountain', 'spring', 'Zen' and 'farm' are all linked to different health systems. "Steep mountain, Lightness cloud, pure water, delicacy furnishings, elegant house, Zen, self-cultivation" are used as auxiliary graphics to enrich the brand image.

山致静，欣然于身

水致净，润泽于心

心致境，通达于灵

峻山

—

steep mountain

淨水

—

clear spring

盈雲

—

lithe cloud

精物

—

nature boutique

皎月

—

bright moon

靈禪

—

zen spirit

雅居

—

elegance house

強身

—

strong body

代 用名
董事长
江西明月山月之泉旅游开发有限公司
Add. 江西省宜春市袁州区温汤镇
矿疗办公楼四楼
Tel. 0795-351 6666 / 138 8888 8888
www.myswq.com
月之泉
MOON SPRING

明月山下
神来之笔
月之泉

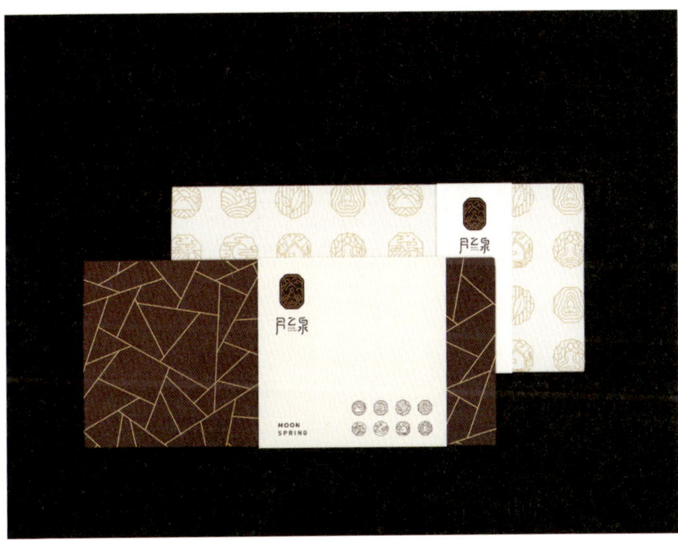
月之泉
月之泉
MOON
SPRING

Reiterative Chinese Character Design

D:
Julio Huang

The reiterative Chinese character postcard design aims to promote the beauty and wisdom of Chinese characters. All of the selected characters are traditional words and symbols of auspiciousness. The visual design of every postcard is based on the character's meaning. Friends and families can guess the character's pronunciation and meaning together as a game while enjoying the beautiful art of Chinese typography.

Techcombank
Mid-Autumn Festival

S:
Bratus

D:
Hung Dinh
Jimmi Tuan
Au Ta

Mid-autumn Festival is a meaningful custom of Asian people in general and the Vietnamese in particular. Techcombank's moon-cake box is designed with combination between traditional and modern culture through decorative patterns on the background of its logo symbol. The cake box recalls the characteristics of the nation and corporate culture in a skillful traditional design, sending customers the best wishes.

TECHCOMBANK

Daimler Financial Services

S:
Paperlux

The studio was asked by Daimler Financial Services to design a unique invitation set and gifts for a trip to three cities. Accordingly, the key visual was designed to be quite modular – there was one for each city as well as one for the whole trip.

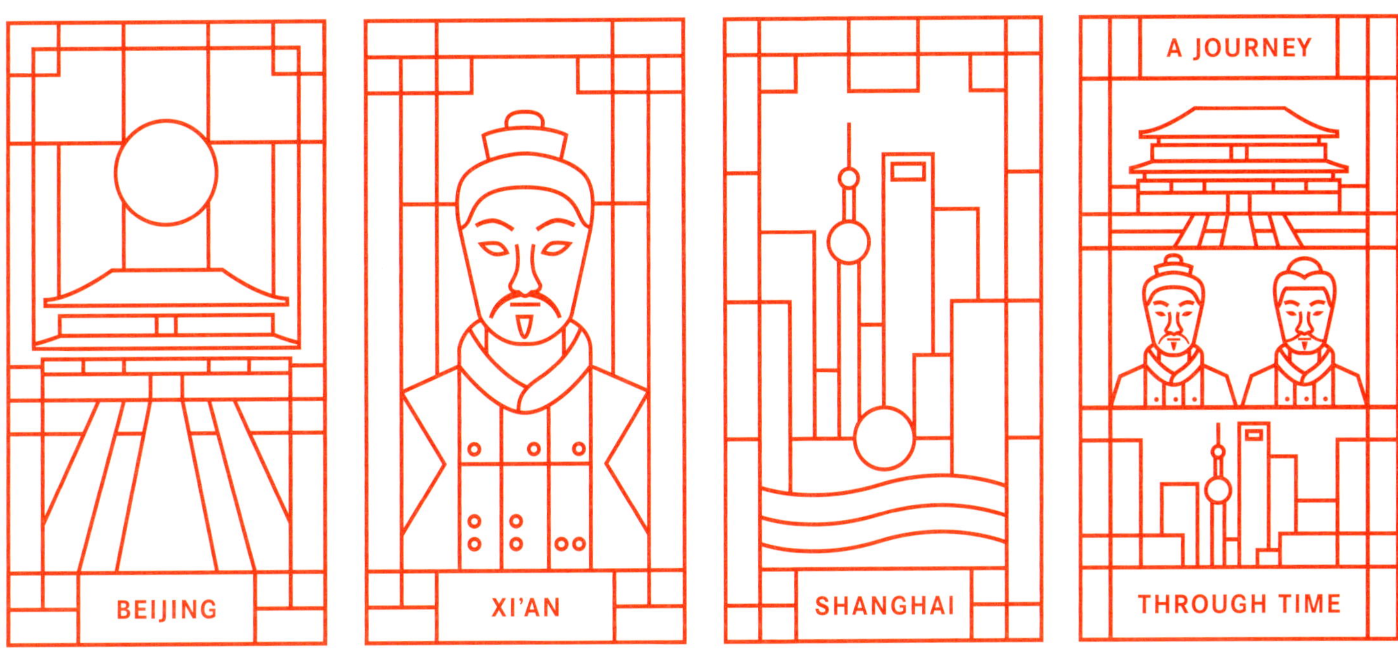
BEIJING
XI'AN
SHANGHAI
A JOURNEY
THROUGH TIME

CHINA
NICE TO MEET YOU

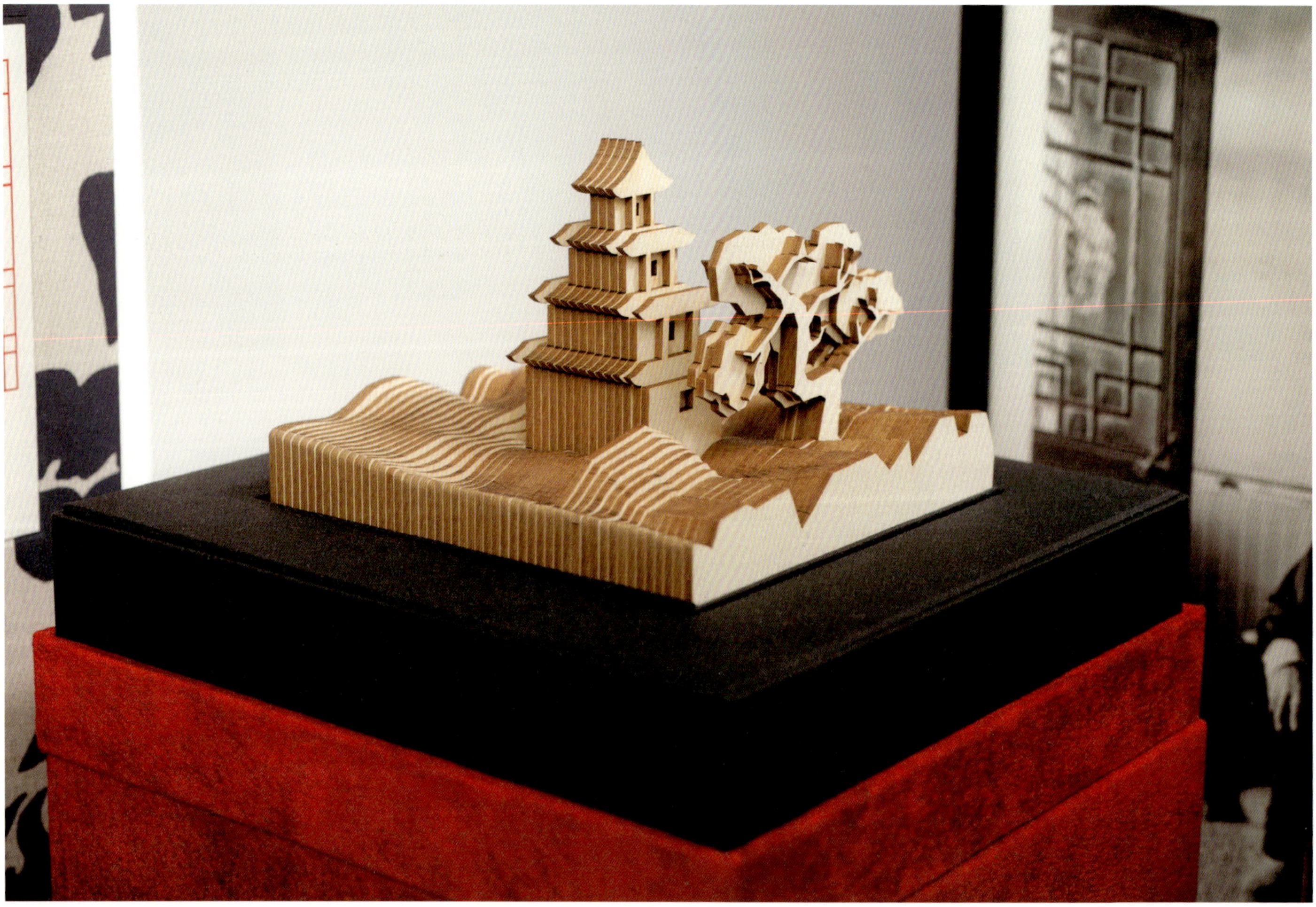

A JOURNEY
THROUGH TIME

ENJOY YOUR AUTHENTIC
CHINESE MEAL

LAN XIA MI Restaurant

D:
Yueming Zheng

Given that the branding is for a seafood restaurant, the designer used sea as the main design element. The auxiliary graphics include different kinds of seafood, adding a sense of vigor and mystery to the brand.

兰
虾
米
LAN XIA MI
RESTAURANT
LAN XIA MI
Restaurant

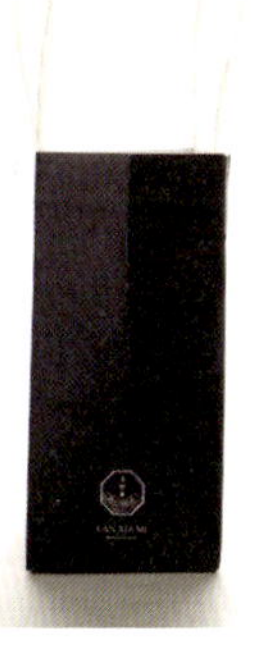

CURA PIZZA

D:
Bohan Shih

CURA means "care" in Italian, which is the central idea of the founder's business philosophy. The four letters CURA combined with the image of Eastern lattice window reflect the exotic culture while being able to relate to local customs.

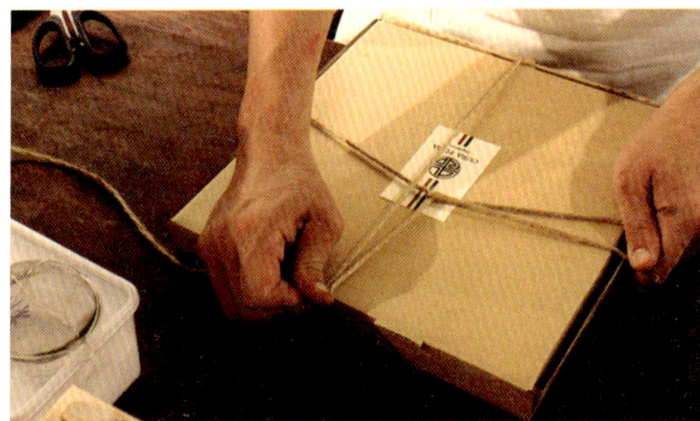

CURA PIZZA

11:00-21:00
每週一店休
02-2339-5877
cura.pizza@gmail.com
cura pizza
10868台北市萬華區東園街68-9號
No.68-9, Dongyuan St., Wanhua Dist.,
Taipei City 108, Taiwan
CURA PIZZA
~Napoletana~

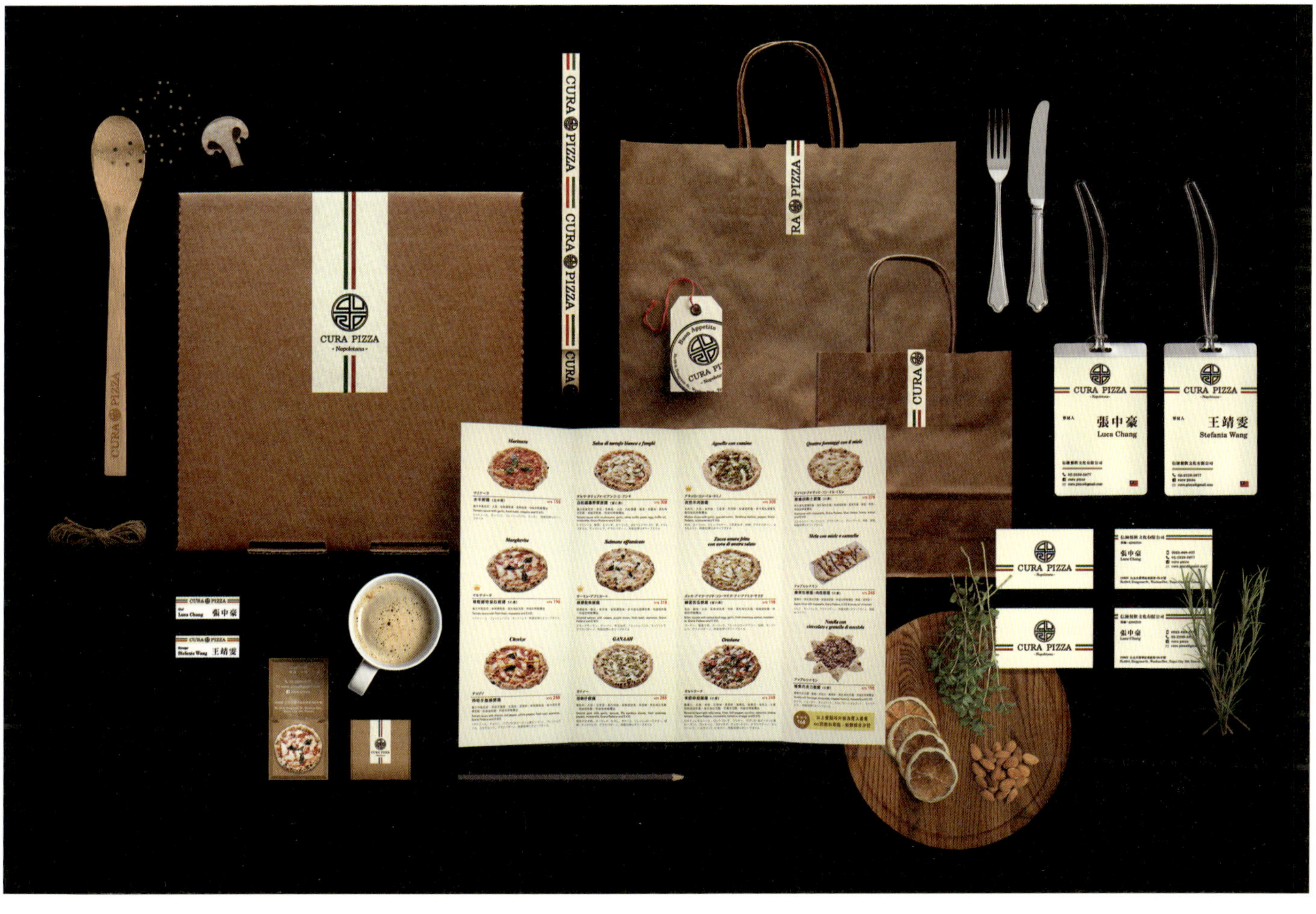

JIUDING

S:
VIM
Graphics
Design

D:
He Yong
Zhang Hui

JIUDING (or the Nine Tripod Cauldrons) was ancient Chinese ritual cauldrons, which is a symbol of power and authority. The design was based on the illustrations in ancient books. The choice of cyan color emphasizes the ancient style of the nine tripod cauldrons, combining traditional and modern styles in a harmonious way.

JIUDING

JIUDING

JIUDING

JIUDING

SHI BI SHOU

D:
Tangyuan Jheng
Menglong Wu

The package designer created an interesting interaction between the inner box and the outer box. When pulling the brightly colored inner boxes out of the hollowed-out outside box, it creates the illusion of a fish with shiny scales swimming. The image of a milkfish was created with the use of traditional Chinese calligraphy.

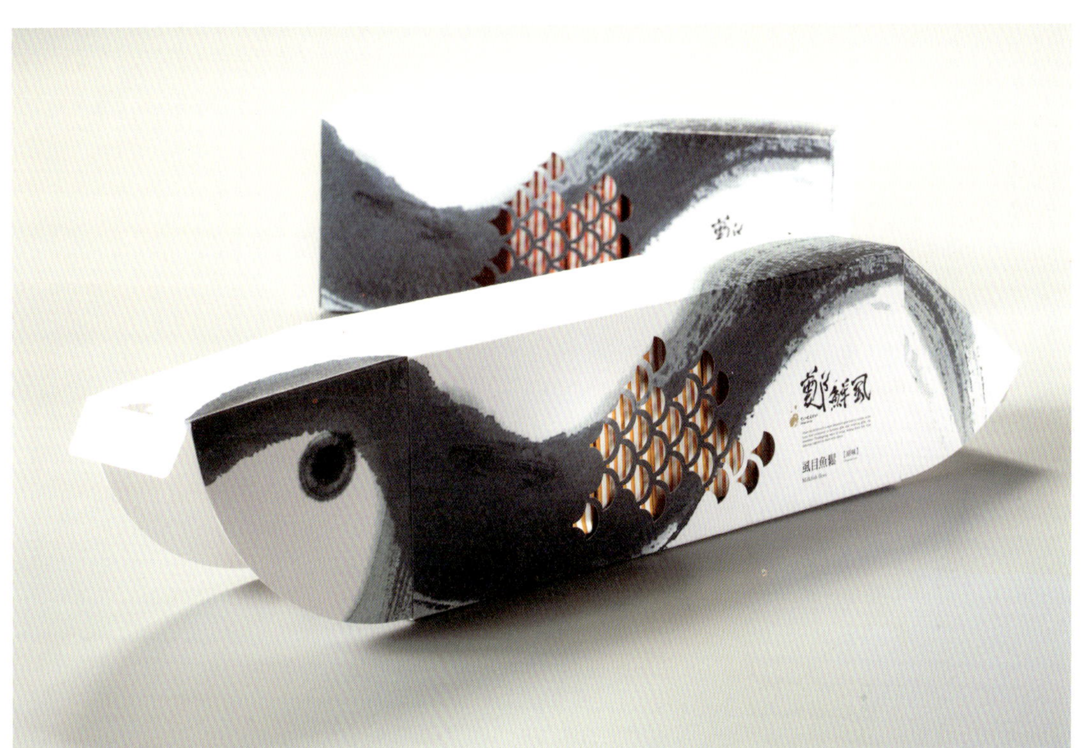

THE ANIMAL MOTIF

The animal motif is one of the most common traditional patterns in China. In the ancient time, people used different animals to symbolize different meanings, reflecting their belief and ideology in different historical backgrounds.

龙 THE CHINESE DRAGON MOTIF

In Chinese myths, dragons traditionally symbolize strong and often auspicious power with particularly control over water, rainfall, lightning and thundering. Ancient Chinese took it as a symbol of imperial authority. The dragon motif has an important role in Chinese motifs and was widely used to decorate the royal palace. Different dragon motifs are still used in various decoration designs in contemporary China. The famous dragon dance in traditional Chinese festivals is one prominent example.

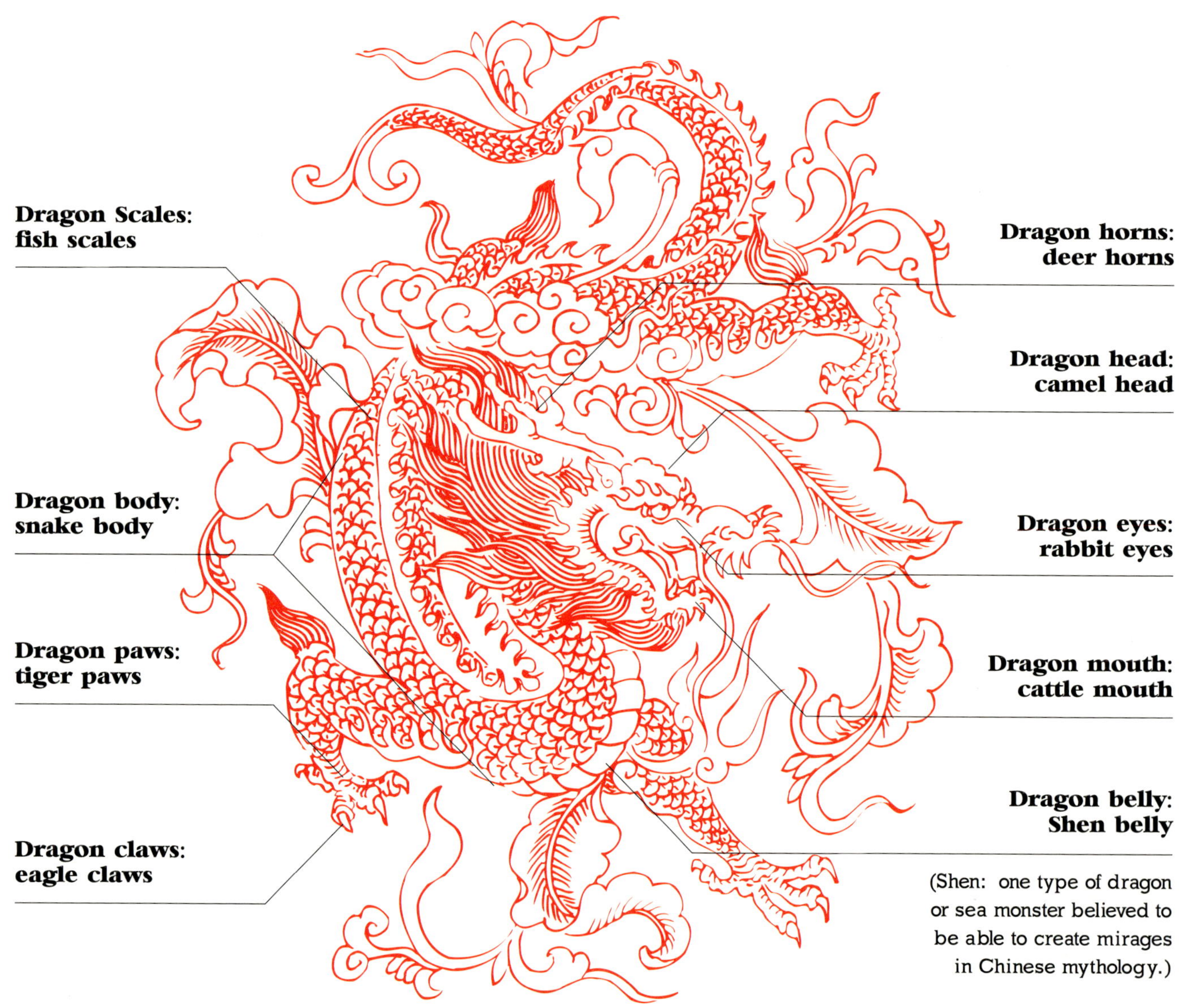

(Shen: one type of dragon or sea monster believed to be able to create mirages in Chinese mythology.)

Elements

The dragons are most commonly depicted as snake-like animals with four legs. The image of the Chinese dragon is made up of body parts from nine animals, namely, the eyes of a rabbit, the horns of a deer, the mouth of a cow, the head of a camel, the belly of Shen, the paws of a tiger, the claws of an eagle, the scales of fish and the body of a snake. The length from its head to the fore limbs, from the fore limbs to the waist and from the waist to the tail is exactly the same.

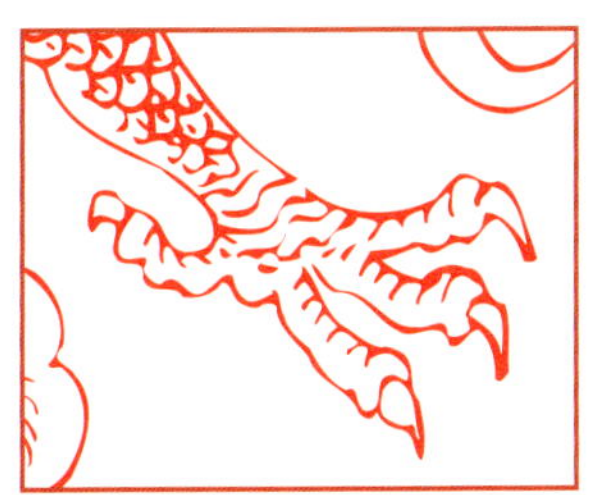

Dragon Claws

The first toe and the second toe shaped like the Chinese character " — ", the triangle-shaped toes displays sharp style.

Dragon mouth

An open mouth with its teeth shown reveals the fierce side of its character

Dragon Scales

The neat crescent-shape scales are a symbol of grace and dinity.

Dragon tail

A robust snake tail displays its intimidating great strength.

Dragon hair

The dragon hair flutter backward.

Dragon Eyes

The big and round eyes display its majestic image.

Auspicious cloud & Scroll grass pattern

The auspicious cloud and scroll grass pattern displays the dragon's mightiness and power.

The phoenix, fenghuang, is an ancient Chinese mythological bird that is believed to reign over all other birds. Like the image of the Chinese dragon, the image of phoenix is a Han ethnic totem. To the Chinese people, it is auspicious and a symbol of high virtue, grace and peace. The phoenix motif is also a symbol of Chinese imperial authority and is often used along with the Chinese dragon motif. The phoenix is said to be subjected to the dragon and its image was used for the decoration of the rooms and clothes of the emperor's wife and concubines.

凤 凰

THE PHOENIX MOTIF

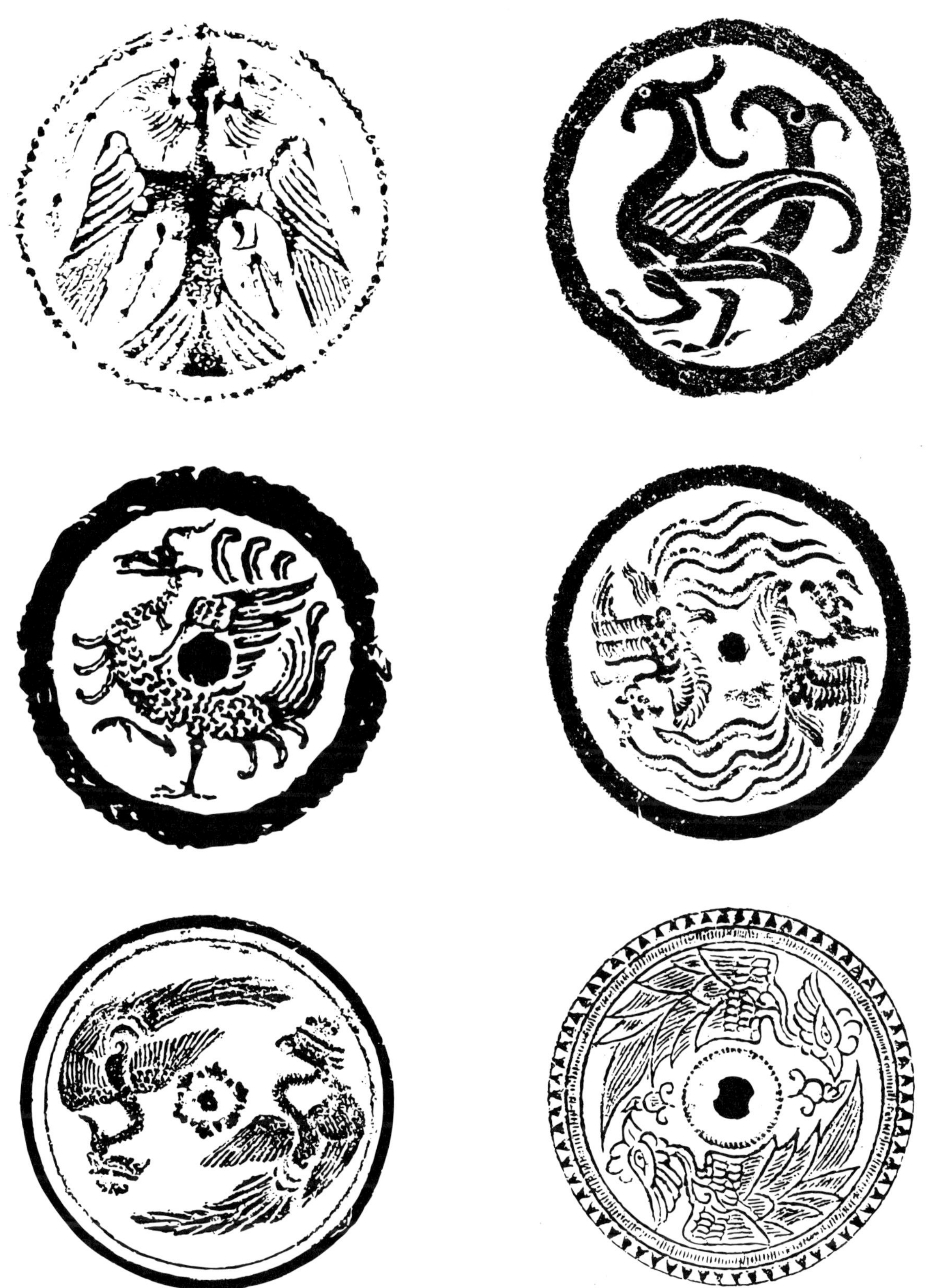

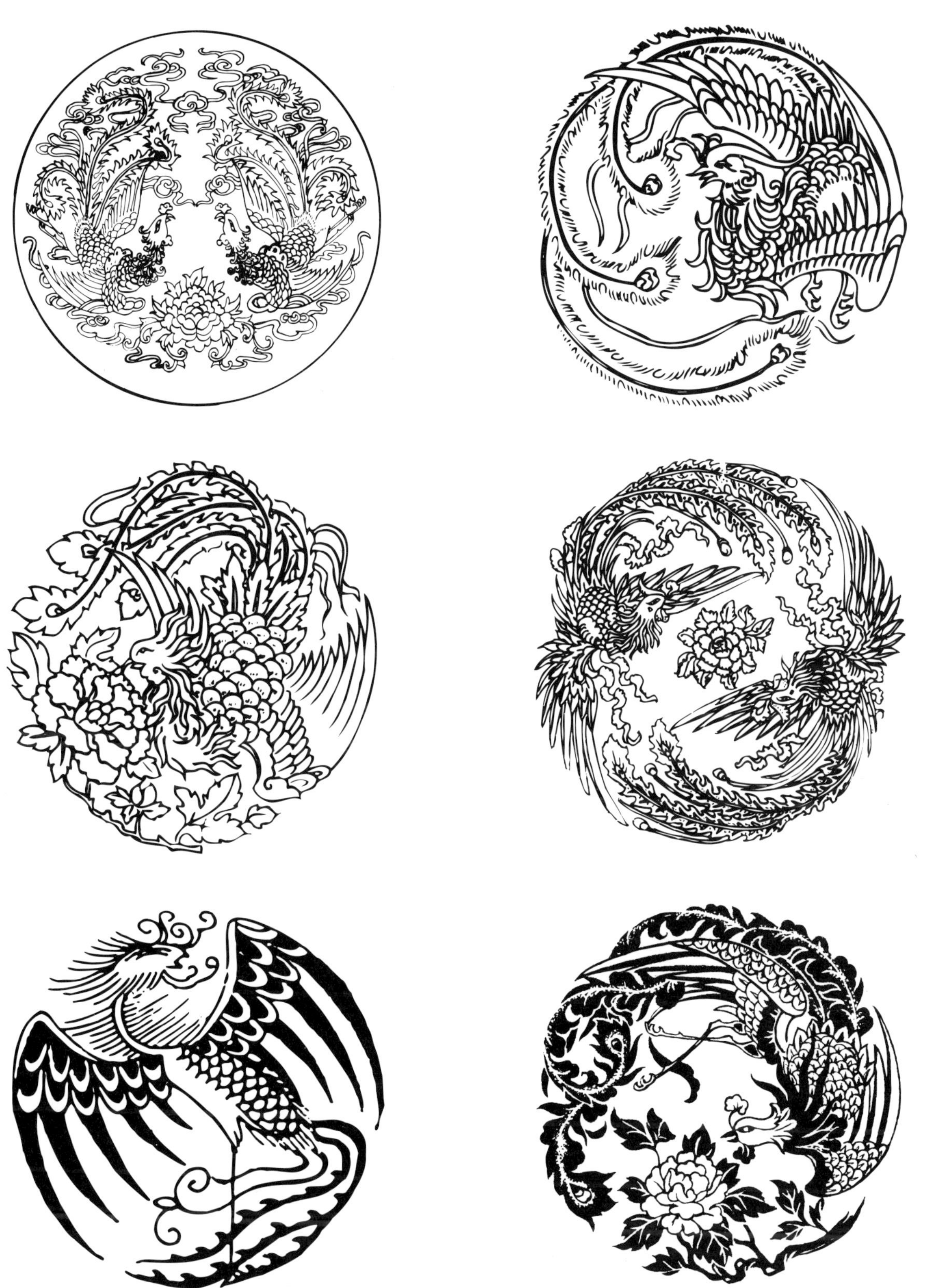

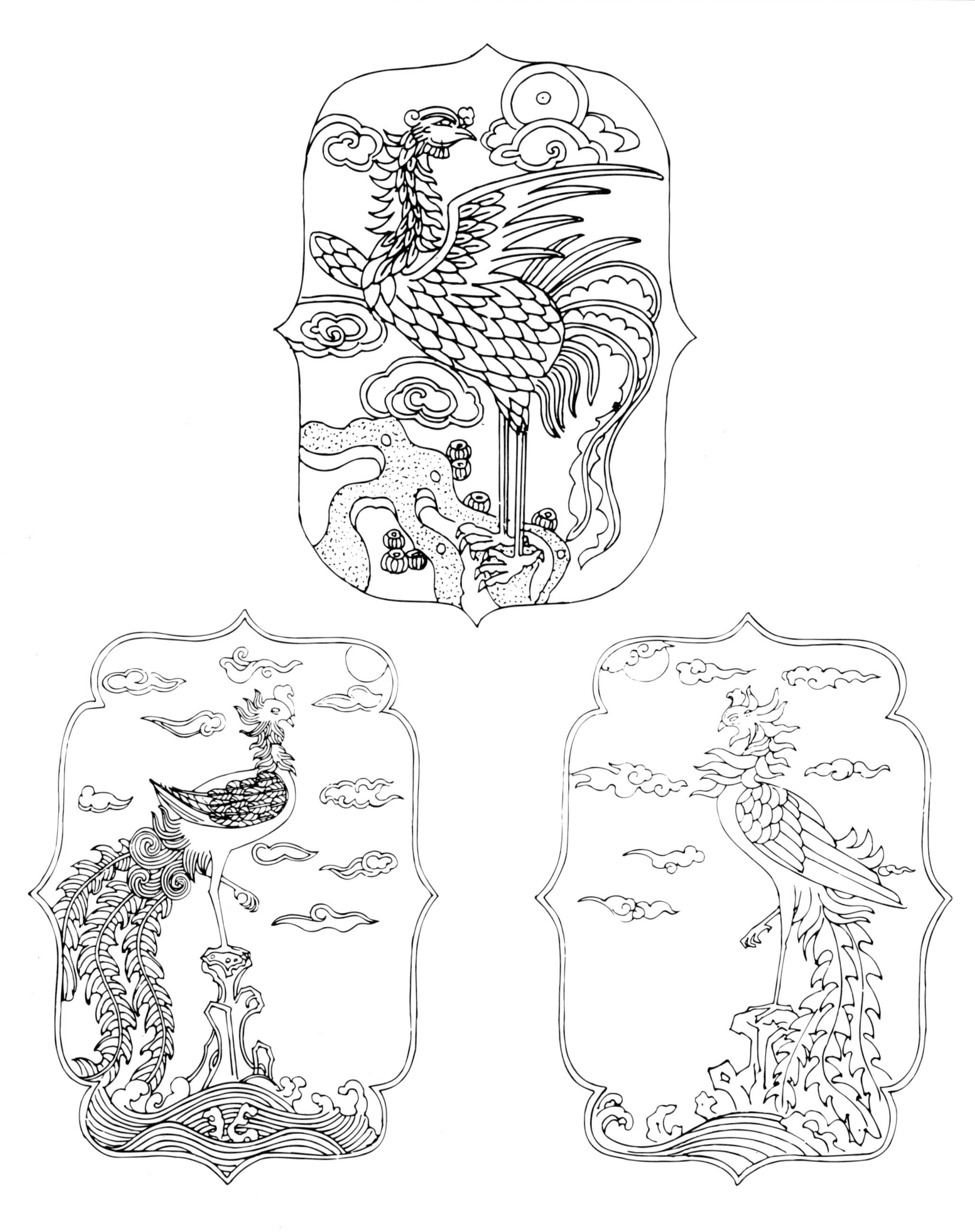

Qilin is a mythical animal in ancient Chinese mythology symbolizing benevolence and auspiciousness. Legend has it that Qilin is gentle and loving. When it walks, it is very careful not to harm or tread on any living thing. The fearsome looking Qilin only punishes the wicked. The appearance of Qilin is considered a good omen that brings harvest, prosperity, longevity and goodness. For its cultural connotation, the Qilin motif is often used in the Chinese folk crafts that are made to be children's jewelry, carrying the wish for safety and happiness for the children. It is believed that Qilin can bring children to a family. The motif of "Qilin Bringing Sons" is a popular design on porcelain art.

THE QILIN MOTIF

The image of crane is a classic porcelain decorative motif. In ancient times, Chinese regarded cranes as fairy cranes. Cranes have high status in Chinese culture. The Redcrowned Crane is a symbol of longevity, auspiciousness and elegance. Being also a symbol of integrity and righteousness, crane motif was often used as a decorative design on the garments of government officials in ancient China.

THE CRANE MOTIF

Fish symbolizes wealth as in Chinese the character for fish " 鱼 " yu , sounds like that of the character " 余 " yu which means abundance and affluence. Fish also signifies marriage and the birth of many children. The most popular fish motif found in Chinese art and culture is that of the Carp or Koi fish. Known to most Westerners as Koi Fish, the Chinese carp has numerous symbolic values in Chinese culture. Carp is a powerful symbol of strength and perseverance.

鱼

THE FISH MOTIF

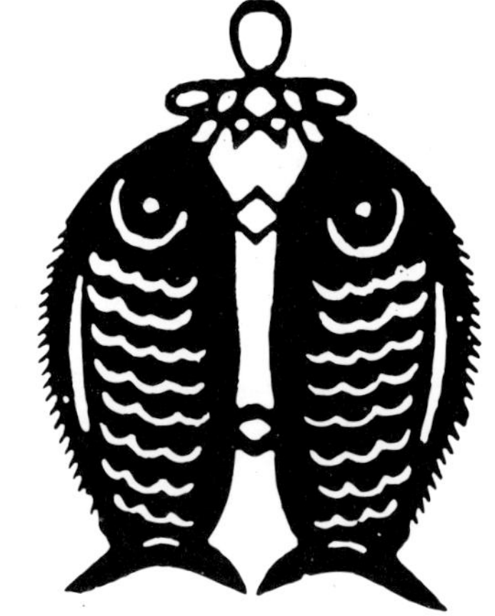

有
貴
富

The bat motif is regarded as a symbol of happiness in traditional Chinese decorative art. Chinese lore describes bat as a symbol of longevity and happiness. The Chinese character for bat " 蝠 " fu sounds identical to the word for good fortune " 福 " fu , making bats popular Chinese rebuses. Five bats together represent the Five Blessings, wufu, namely, longevity, wealth, health, the love of virtue and a peaceful death. Bat motif can often be found in many ancient buildings and carved art objects.

蝙 蝠

THE BAT MOTIF

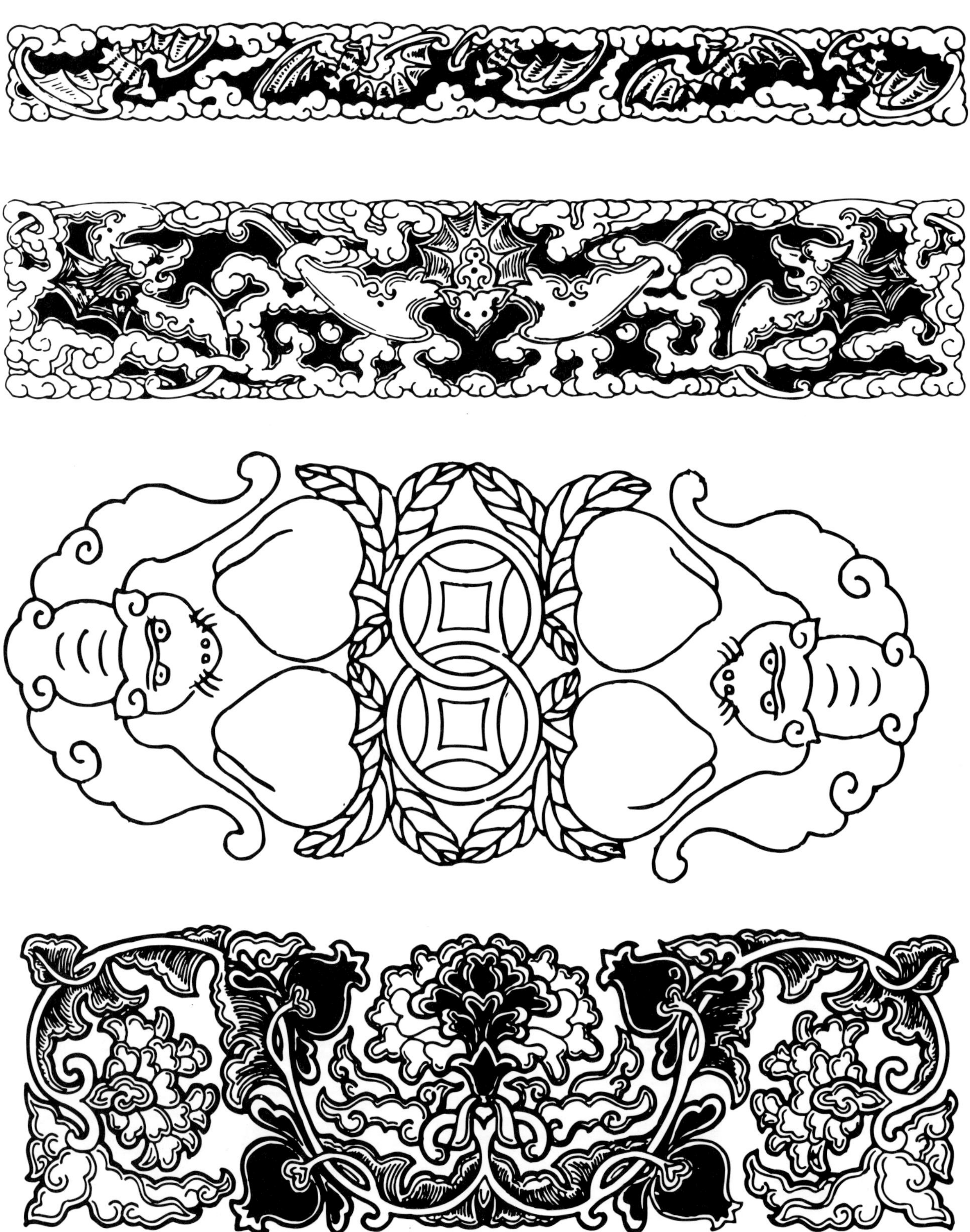

WELL-DONE HEALTHY WINE

S:
UNIDEA BANK

D:
Zhang Xiaoming
Chen Yue
Ou Yanrong
Huang Renqiang
Liu Danghua
Yang Guang
Qian Jianfu

WELL-DONE HEALTHY WINE is an inheritance of Taoist health theory. It is of great help to improve human body function and keep inner balance. The four illustrations on the package indicate the different functions of the wine with each illustration tells a classical story.

健康長寿
丹道养生

道家秘传
中华丹道养生
強身健体
丹道养生
華丹
强身健体
道家秘傳
中華丹道養生
強身健體
華丹

華丹

華丹

Red Envelope for Lunar New Year

D:
Giang Ong

Nowadays, many children do not know and understand what the Tet (the Lunar New Year in Vietnam) is. All they know is that on the Tet holiday they can receive lucky money and they use the money to buy stuffs. Therefore, the designer chose to use the Red Envelope to tell a short story to help them understand the traditional holiday.

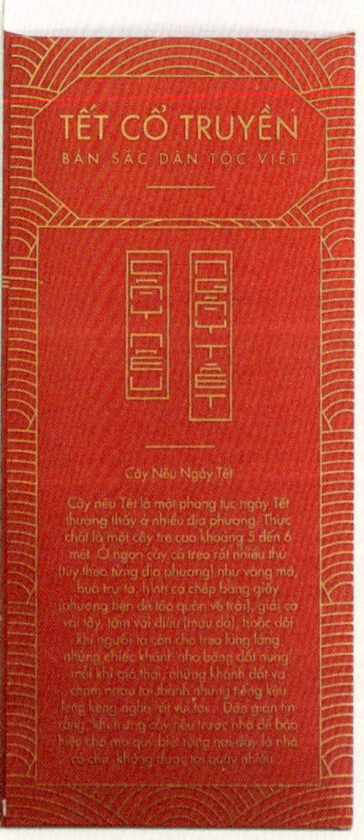

TẾT CỔ TRUYỀN
BẢN SẮC DÂN TỘC VIỆT
Xuất Hành và Hái Lộc

TẾT CỔ TRUYỀN

FENG HE

S:
1983 ASIA

D:
SU SU & YAO

FENG HE is an independent high-end Chinese home decoration brand. In Chinese culture, 'Wind' is an abstract phenomenon of airflow. It also embodies the Chinese people's wisdom and elegance. Crane is a symbol of longevity, good luck and elegance. 1983 ASIA combined abstract and figurative representation technique of expression and designed a soft cursive font. This design adds a sense of oriental charm to the brand image.

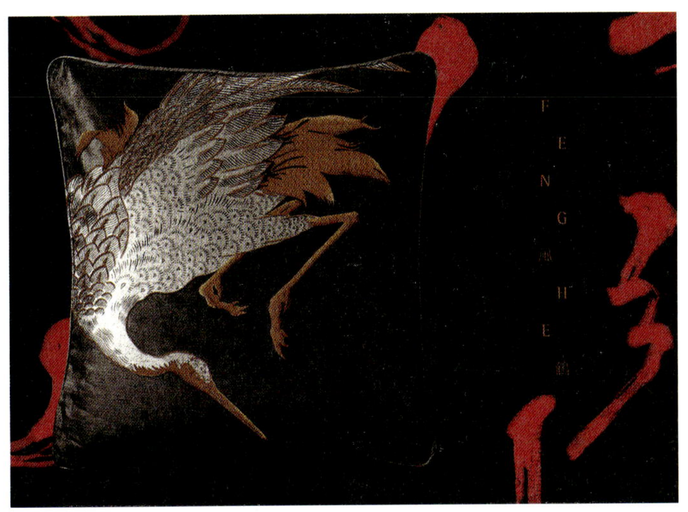

Peranakan Hipwrap Sarong

D:
Zilin Yee

The Peranakan is a mixture of Chinese and Malay culture. The story of Peranakan tells how Chinese migrants settled and started their own families with the local Malays. To keep the Peranakan spirit alive for future generations, the Baba Nyonya Heritage Museum in Malacca, intend to revive the Batik Sarong as part of the unique Peranakan traditions. The design objective of this project is to promote the "Peranakan Batik Sarong" as an exquisite Peranakan heritage collector's item.

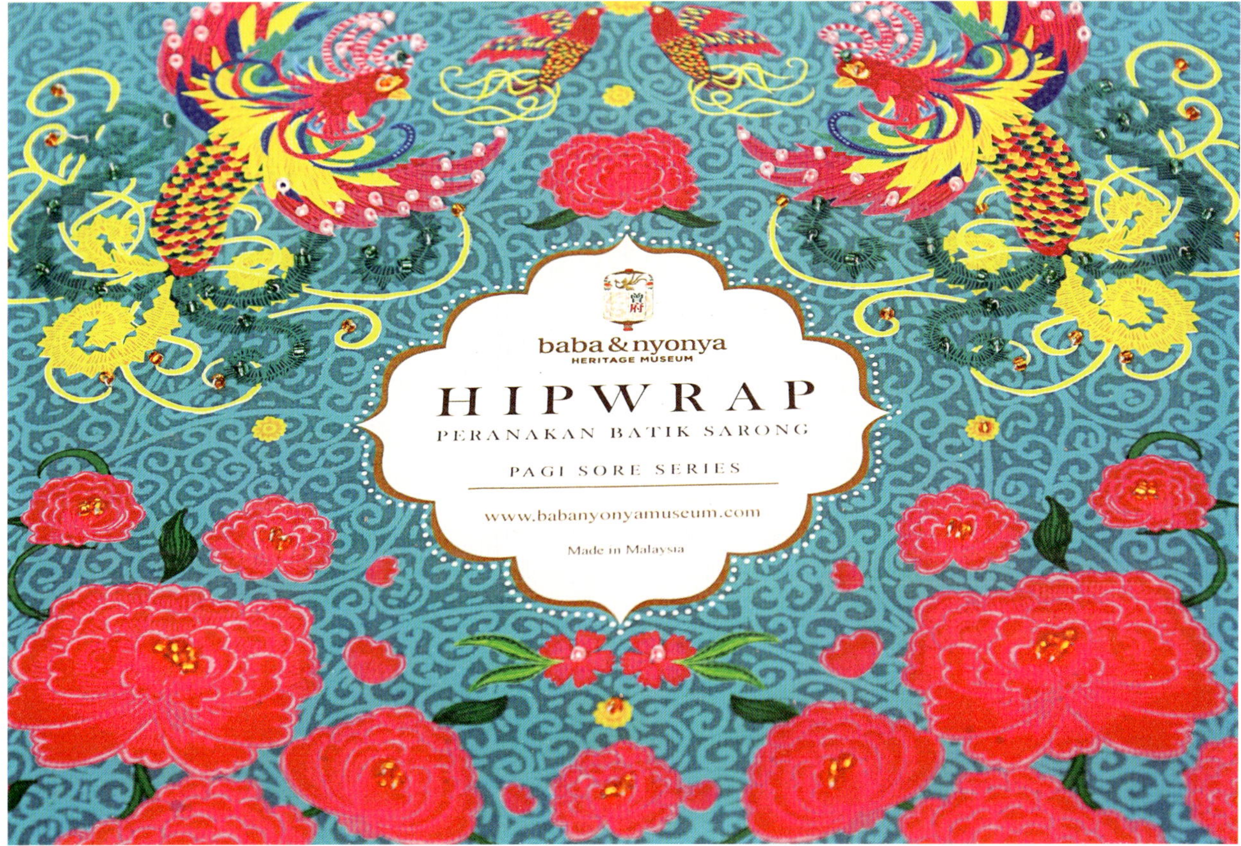
baba&nyonya
HERITAGE MUSEUM
HIPWRAP
PERANAKAN BATIK SARONG
PAGI SORE SERIES
www.babanyonyamuseum.com
Made in Malaysia

The Feast Board Game

D:
Khoa Ha

The Feast Board Game is a popular traditional Vietnamese game often played during Lunar New Year.The use of oriental auspicious motif as an auxiliary pattern indicates the good luck in the coming new year. The designer used iconic Vietnamese imagery in a revamped way to create an integration between the aesthetics of oriental culture and western culture.

BẦU
CUA
TÔM
CÁ
"THE FEAST"

CÁ
"THE FEAST"
a traditional dice game
to celebrate the new year
with good things to come
4+ PLAYERS
FAMILY
AGE 6+

RULES OF PLAY
4-10
GOOD LUCK

CÁ
"THE FEAST"

4+ PLAYERS
FAMILY
AGE 6+

Ginger Restaurant

S:
C&S Brand

"Ginger" is a new Cantonese restaurant. The designers created a personality for the brand: a yuppie who is manful, stable but natural, self-regulating but free. They captured the visual images from the character and selected 'Kylin' as the core symbol of the brand. The English brand name was written in traditional Chinese calligraphy.

G I N G E R

MENU
Ginger
GINGER

GINGER

Ginger
Ginger

Ginger

不止新派粵菜
Ginger

GINGER
GINGER
GINGER

ZEN

S:
1983 ASIA

D:
SU SU & YAO

The design for this home decoration brand made use of traditional home decorative elements such as the "five-color auspicious clouds" and "Ru Yi" (a curved decorative object), aiming to create a unique modern brand image that restores the lost glory of traditional homes.

珍 ZEN·PADAUK 眞

珍 ZEN·PADAUK 真

珍 ZEN·PADAUK 真

ZEN·PADAUK

PLANTS AND FLOWERS MOTIF

Plants and Flowers motifs are included in Chinese auspicious patterns. Ancient Chinese believed that every kind of plants and flowers has its own symbolic meaning. The plants and flowers motifs reflect the customs, cultures and aesthetic values in ancient China.

梅　花 **Plum Blossom**

兰　花 **Orchid**

竹　子 **Bamboo**

菊　花 **Chrysanthemum**

The Four Noble Ones, in Chinese art, refers to four plants: orchid, bamboo, chrysanthemum, and plum blossom. The term compares the four plants to Confucianist junzi , or "gentlemen". Orchids symbolize modesty, beauty, joy and purity. Bamboo remains strong, honest, and true to its principles. Chrysanthemum reminds people that it is possible to triumph when the going gets tough and to be brave when faced with adversity. Plum blossom defies winter and blooms, representing the hope for the return of spring.

四君子——梅兰竹菊

THE FOUR NOBLE ONES MOTIF

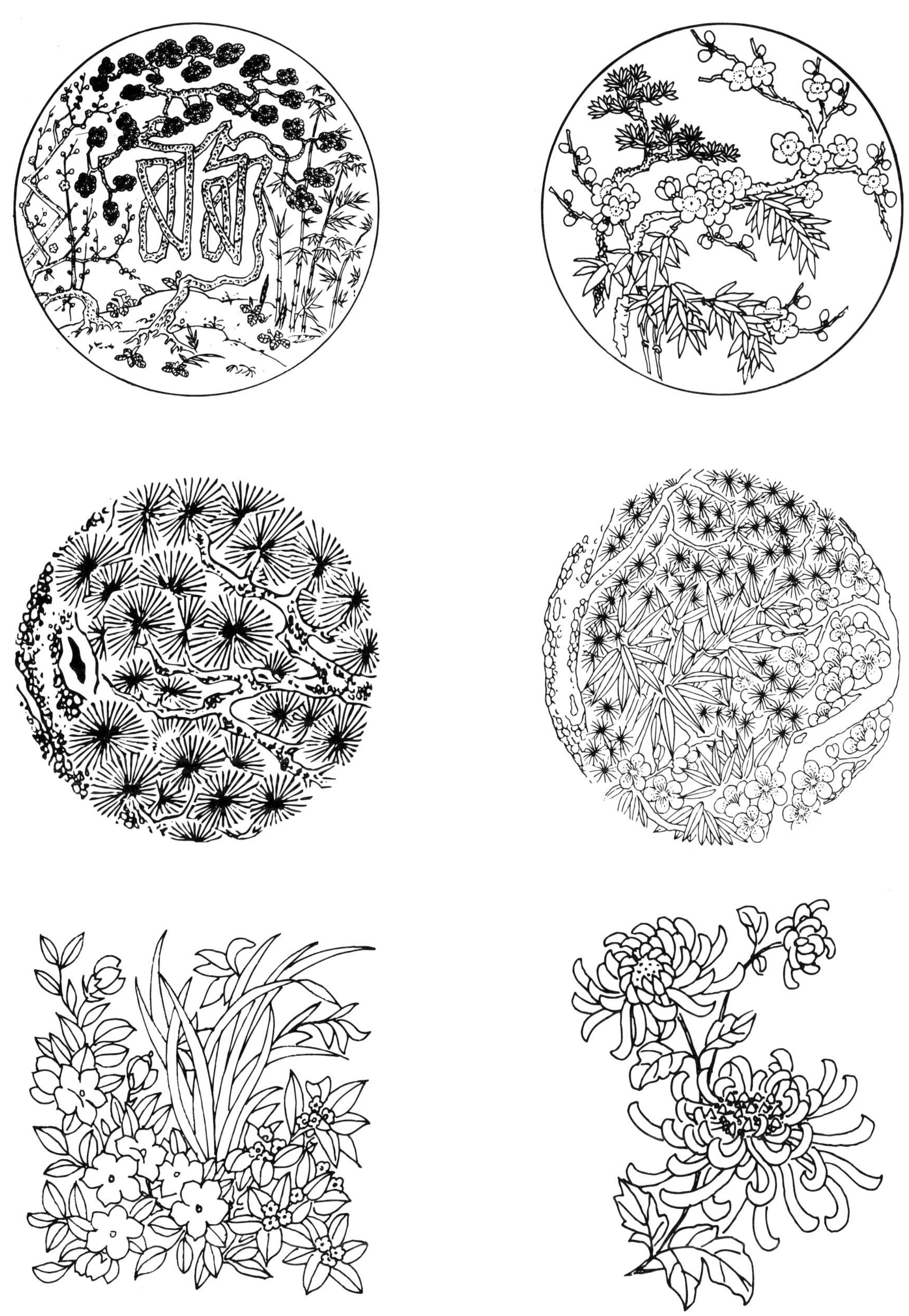

Peony has compound, deeply lobed leaves, and large, often fragrant flowers. With the title "the Queen of All Flowers", it has long been regarded as a symbol of riches and honors. As one of the traditional floral motifs, the peony motif is widely used in various porcelain designs.

牡 丹

THE PEONY MOTIF

Lotus has often been used as a symbolic plant in some religions and philosophies. It represents divinity, the virtues of female sexual purity and non-attachment. In China, lotus flower is honored as the flower of righteous men. It symbolizes an ideal personality in traditional Chinese culture. One lotus seed head carries many seeds, which makes lotus also a symbol of strong fertility. The lotus flower motif is usually used in apparel and utensil designs.

莲 花

THE LOTUS FLOWER MOTIF

HANAMIKOJI

S:
SUMP DESIGN

D:
Zihuai Shen

The name of the handmade shoes brand "Hanamikoji" was taken from the name of a street in Kyoto, Japan. The use of antique Japanese "wood lattice" in the graphics brings forth the beautiful and delicate style of Kyoto. The logotype design of brand features the graceful posture of Japanese Geisha.

花見小路
hana-
mikoji

Chinese Lunar Calendar Redesign

D:
Chris Chu
Yang Yang

The designers created graphic symbols for the Chinese twenty-four solar terms, traditional festivals, Chinese sexagenary cycle, and the Chinese auspicious days, aiming to let more people know about the Chinese lunar calendar. The red and blue colors create a striking contrast.

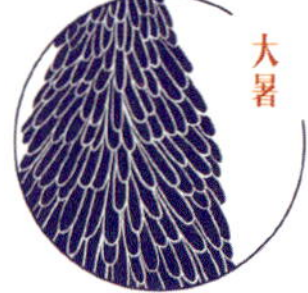

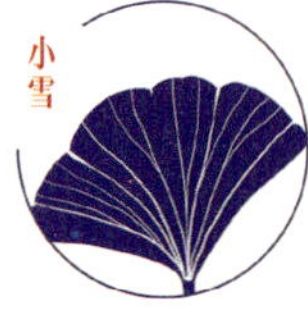

傳統節日
TRADITIONAL FESTIVAL

Pu'er Caky Tea
2014-2016

D:
Yufang Huang

The designers created a new look for the traditional wrappings of cakey tea while preserving the charm of traditional culture. The theme of the packaging design is Chinese homophonic greetings. Two colors and two Chinese greetings were selected to go with traditional totems and calligraphy. The illustrations also help present a lively image of Pu'er tea.

>> patterns of 2014~16'
> 14'
福到
好事
bat > good fortune
persimmon > good thing
> 15'
吉祥
旺來
sheep > lucky
pineapple > thriving
> 16'
有餘
利至
fish > surplus
litchi > benefit

福到
祥
利至
普洱【生茶】二百克
刮風寨小喬木
普洱茶【熟茶】
四百克 布朗山古樹
旺來
丙申
普洱【熟茶】二百克
老曼峨
好事

有餘
丙申
普洱【熟茶】二百克
老班章
好事

THE HAPPY 8

S:
1983 ASIA

D:
SU SU & YAO

THE HAPPY 8 is a high-end chained-hotel brand in Malaysia. The brand image was inspired by the combination of Nanyang culture and art. The vibrant colors are a reflection of local culture while the multi-cultural background of the brand is highlighted through the illustrations.

TheHappy
Eight

TheHappy
Eight

發

The Happy
Eight

Eight

Eight

The Happy
Eight

Qing He Wu

D:
Gu long

The main products of the brand "Qing He Wu" are tea, chinaware, cloth and photos. The brand image is consisted of lotus, Chinese characters and tea sets, highlighting its Oriental cultural background and Zen style.

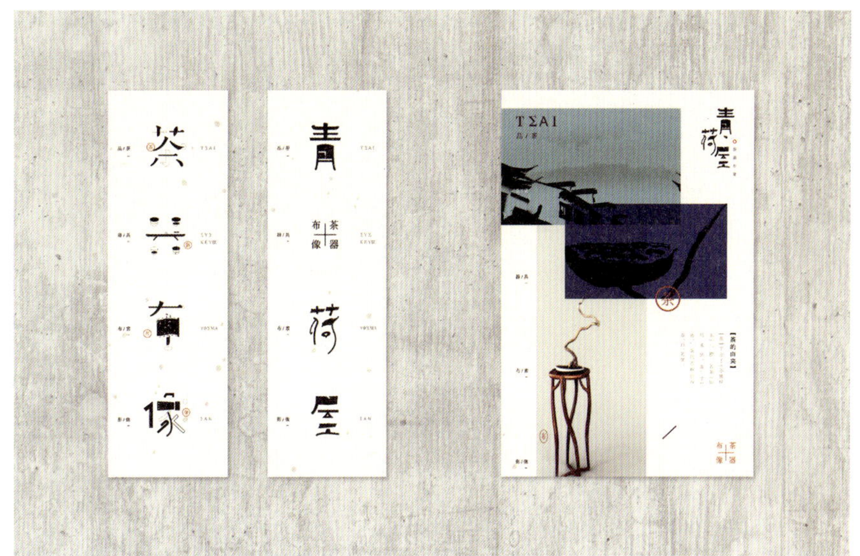
TΣAI
青荷屋
布 茶 像 器

TΣAI

TΣAI
ΣΥΣ KEYΞ
ΥΦΣΜΑ
ΣΑΝ

INDEX

Khoa Ha

www.khoaha.com
208

Victor Design

www.victad.com.tw
056

Lee chie-hting

www.behance.net/leechiehting
082

VIM Graphics Design

www.59ilogo.com.cn
036 146

Paperlu

www.paperlux.com
138

Y.STUDIO / Ziji Yu

www.behance.net/JOE-YU
061

SUMP DESIGN / Zihuai Shen

www.sumpdesign.com
078 240

Yueming Zheng

www.behance.net/yuemingstudio
142

Tangyuan Jheng

www.behance.net/4a0j2049490a
150

Yufang Huang

www.behance.net/letterofcat
244

UNIDEA BANK

www.behance.net/UnideaBank
198

Zilin Yee

www.zilinyee.wixsite.com/zilinyee
206

ACKNOWLEDGEMENTS

We would like to thank all the designers and contributors who have been involved in the production of this book; their contributions have been indispensable to its creation. We would also like to express our gratitude to all the producers for their invaluable opinions and assistance throughout this project. And to the many others whose names are not credited but have made helpful suggestions, we thank you for your continuous support.

FUTURE COOPERATIONS

If you wish to participate in SendPoints' future projects and publications, please send your website or portfolio to editor01@sendpoints.cn.